Conscious Living

Conscious Living

A Guidebook
for Spiritual Transformation

Swami Rama

Himalayan Institute Hospital Trust
Swami Rama Nagar, P.O. Doiwala,
Distt. Dehradun 248140, Uttaranchal, India

Originally published as *A Personal Philosophy of Life.*
© 2002 by the Himalayan Institute Hospital Trust

Editing: Prakash Keshaviah
Cover design: Connie Gage

First USA edition, 2002
Printed in the United States of America
ISBN 8-190100-47-5
Library of Congress Control Number 2002105137

Published by:

Himalayan Institute Hospital Trust
Swami Rama Nagar, P.O. Doiwala
Distt. Dehradun 248140, Uttaranchal, India
Tel: 91-135-412068, Fax: 91-135-412008
hihtsrc@sancharnet.in; www.hihtindia.org

Distributed by:
Lotus Press
P.O. Box 325
Twin Lakes, WI 53181
www.lotuspress.com
lotuspress@lotuspress.com
800-824-6396

Contents

Acknowledgments

We wish to express our gratitude to the Sindhu Mandir for hosting Swamiji's lectures in Singapore, to Mohan and Shanta Ramchand for recording the lectures, to Wesley Van Linda for editing the audio taped lecture series and for assisting with the production of this book, and to Connie Gage for designing the cover.

Foreword

This is a practical book for people living in the world. The word 'practical' implies that the teaching can be practiced in the world, in the midst of family, career and social obligations. No prior preparation is required for reading this book, and after reading this book, no further teaching is required. If one were to sincerely practice the teachings presented by H.H. Shri Swami Rama in this book, one will surely achieve the goal of self realization, a state described by Swamiji as the summum bonum of life, a state of bliss, a state of perfection.

This book is based on nine lectures delivered by Swamiji in Singapore in 1991 and 1992. The lectures were audio-taped, transcribed, edited and re-organized into the nine chapters of this book. Six of the nine lecture tapes are also being made available as a separate audio book. In editing this book, great care has been taken to preserve the spontaneity of Swamiji's style of teaching. This has been done even at the risk of offending purists of grammar and syntax. As you turn the pages of this book, we want you to feel Swamiji's presence, savour his words and bathe in his joy.

In his very practical approach to life, Swamiji teaches us how to preserve health and prevent disease by making the body a fit instrument for achieving the purpose of life.

Swamiji, therefore, starts with the four primitive fountains of food, sleep, self-preservation, and sex, the body, and the breath, before delving deeper into the mind, emotions and personal relationships. He concludes the book by describing four paths of spiritual practice, any of which can be adopted, depending on one's temperament, to reach the goal of self realization. The four paths are those of prayer, contemplation, meditation and selfless action. In most cases, a synthesis of the four paths can quicken one's progress on the path.

Swamiji stresses throughout the book, that one only needs to take ten to twenty minutes, twice a day, to practice a simple regimen that includes proper posture, proper breathing, progressive relaxation and meditation. Though simple, regular practice of these techniques will allow us to experience the stillness of body, breath, senses, mind and emotions, this stillness emanating from deep within us, from the *atman* or soul. This stillness will insulate us from the turmoil and stresses of worldly life and allow us to function creatively, skillfully, selflessly and lovingly in the world. This stillness will become our constant companion, reminding us that God dwells in us and we are all living shrines of the Divine. As Swamiji remarks, "The greatest miracle is that infinity dwells in you. You are a finite vessel and you are carrying infinity in you. It's the greatest of all wonders."

Prakash Keshaviah, Ph.D., Editor
21 May 2001
Himalayan Institute Hospital Trust
Jolly Grant, Dehradun, India

CHAPTER ONE

A Personal Philosophy of Life

I have come to share my joy truthfully with you. I say, ye human beings, among all the species on the earth, you are the greatest. You are the greatest for you can change your destiny, you can build your destiny, you can enlighten yourself. Other species do not have this privilege. From among the kingdom of animals, the kingdom of vegetables, the kingdom of rocks and clay you alone have that privilege. Why are you not enjoying that privilege? I have come to remind you of that. Have you seen guards at night? They roam around and say, "Remain awake, remain awake!" But you remain sleeping. I am like that guard. *Uttishtata, uttishtata!* Wake up, wake up! *Jagrata,* remain awake. *Prapta varanya bodhasa,* gain knowledge. This is my message to everybody. I know they are sleeping but yet I have to say this. This is my duty. This is my job. If I don't do it, I will not be happy. We human beings, all of us, have the birthright to attain the final goal of life, and sooner or later we'll reach that goal. So, everyone has hopes. But do you have the patience to wait for such a long time? I don't.

I will try to cover the entire philosophy of life in these lectures. We need to understand one word and that is called freedom — freedom from all bondages, from all ignorance. That state which is free from stress, strain, bondage and ignorance is called the state of enlighten-ment and that can be considered to be the state of perfec-tion.

What is the aim and goal of life? You think I am going to tell you it's God? No, that's not being practical. The aim of life is contentment and for that you need ad-justment. Can you adjust yourself mentally, physically, and through speech so that you are content? What do you mean by being content? I always say: do not be sat-isfied yet remain content. Contentment is a great virtue that you can develop in your daily life. If it is not there, your God business is not going to help you, let me as-sure you. Repeating God, God, God, God, God, without understanding! What a waste of time and energy! I am not an atheist, but I have learned to analyze things with clarity of mind and that's how I was trained. And that same thing I am imparting to you now.

You may say that the purpose of life is to attain God. I say no. In my childhood, one day I went to my Master, a great yogi and sage from Bengal, who lived in the Himalayas for many, many years. And I said, "My heart cries because you have not shown me God. And so I think you have destroyed my life." He kept quiet. He said, "Go on." I said, "I want to see God." He re-sponded, "You want to see God? Are you sure you want to see God?" I said, "Yes." He said, "I will show you God in the morning, tomorrow morning." So that whole night I remained restless and I could not sleep. I was filled with joy but at times doubts too came into my mind. I could not sleep. In the morning, without sleep, I was looking tired. I took my bath and that day I be-came an extraordinarily holy person bowing often in front of my Master because he was going to show me God. He said, "What has happened to you today? Your behavior has changed." I said, "It's because I want to see God today." He said, "I promised to show you God. I will be very honest, but will you please also be honest with me?" I said, "Yes." He asked me a question, "Tell me what kind of God do you want to see?" I was taken aback and asked, "Are there many kinds of God?" He said, "No. I want to know what is the concept of God in your mind?"

All your life you long to meet God, but you have no concept of God. What type of God will you meet? Everyone says, "I want to see God, I want to see God." Someone is doing chanting, someone is meditating, someone is talking of Gita, someone is talking of Upanishads. Nobody sees God, it's all mere talk. Why? Because you don't have a clear concept. You should have a clear concept and then you should learn to work towards that concept. Only then will you get it.

So I said to my Master, "It means you bluffed me yesterday. You promised that you would show me God. And this morning you say what kind of God do you want to see?" He replied, "Look, I promised to show you the kind of God you wanted to see. Think about it. I give you time. At any time you can come and say that this is the type of God I want to see and I'll show you that God." I was speechless. So is the case with all of you. You want to see God without knowing what He is and that's why He never appears before you. If He suddenly appears before you, perhaps you will not recognize Him. So if there is no clarity of mind, if there is no purity of heart, your whole life remains full of confusion. This is my point. What do you mean by seeing God? Are you at peace, are you happy, do you lead a balanced life, are you attaining your goal in life? These are the vital questions of life.

So after half an hour, my Master again called out to me, "Have you decided what kind of God you want to see?" I said, "Not yet." He said, "Please decide and come to me and I will show you." To this day I don't dare to say that I have.

If a swami, a priest or a yogi comes to you, if your teacher or guru comes to you and says, "My child, what do you want? What do you want to know?" There are many things in your mind and heart. You want to become millionaire but you won't tell him. You'll say, "I want to see God." You want to have a good wife but you won't say that. You'll say, "I want to see God." There is a beautiful saying, any human being who gives responsibilities to the Lord, his own responsibilities, cripples human potentials. If you don't want to perform your duties and then say God will do everything for me, this is not good. You are not utilizing the gifts given to you by Providence.

If I have no understanding of what God is, I cannot get enlightened, I can never see God. Even though I have a desire to see God, nothing is going to happen. Let us not cheat ourselves. There are things which we have been repeating without understanding why we are doing it. Tell me what is the purpose of God in your daily life? When you need food, you don't eat God. When you want to wear clothes, you need clothes, not God. Where do we need God in life? Let us understand things rightly.

This human life is very precious. It's not like animal life. Animal activities are completely controlled by nature. They cannot do anything. In the animal kingdom, nothing is by choice. But as a human being, you can do tremendous things, you can perform wonders. You have choice and the power to change. As easily as you can turn your face from this side to that side, you can change yourself. You can transform your personality completely. It's a very simple thing, provided you are practical and you are truthful to yourself. We human beings live our lives based on how the world judges us. Take the case of a wife at home who looks toward her husband all the time, like a German shepherd, wanting to know what he thinks of her. And if he says, "Honey, you look very beautiful, you are wonderful." She may feel, "He has made my day." She leans on him all the time seeking approval. This great force on earth, called womankind, has never been utilized properly. It is only being exploited. And that is one of the causes of our suffering. Please, please, try to understand what I am saying.

I want to give you a glimpse of your individual self, because there are many false notions. When a human being suffers, the suffering is not because of external forces, not because of others. The suffering is because of his or her own thinking and understanding. So we will discuss that. We have many such fears in our life. We talk of God so much, we sing *kirtans*, we study the scriptures like the Ramayana, the Gita and Bible, we go to temples or churches. Yet our ignorance remains. There is no change in our daily life, in our behavior. What is the reason? The reason is that right from our childhood, we are trained to see and examine things in the external world. Nobody teaches us how to look within, find within, and see within. So we remain a stranger to ourselves, yet we want to know others; isn't this strange?

So first of all, a human being should learn to understand himself on all levels and then he can understand all, the Self of all. And he can understand that absolute Self which is called absolute Truth. This is the right system and there are three schools, and any of these

schools will help you: the school of meditation, the
school of contemplation, and the school of prayer. If
you learn to understand prayer, what prayer is, you
can easily evoke your emotional self and attain that
height of ecstasy and be there. If you understand the
philosophy of life through contemplation you can attain the goal of life. If you understand the school of meditation and systematically meditate, you can attain the
fourth state which is called sleepless sleep, you can attain the purpose of life. But if you practice meditation
for a few days, contemplation for a few days, and then
prayer for a few days, and finally decide that none of
them suits you, you won't attain anything. The basic
thing is that we create certain problems and barriers
for ourselves, because of our fears and confusion. We
have certain questions in our mind and we should learn
to tackle them first. As long as you remain under the
pressure of fears you cannot do anything. And talking
about God is a good pastime, but you don't get anything. You may become godly but you cannot attain
God, you cannot have peace, you cannot have happiness. Forgive me if I am crushing your sentiments but
this is the truth.

Let us learn to enjoy one thing. All the great scriptures of the world, which have been revealed to the sages
from the depths of their deep contemplation, say one and
the same thing. A human being has been created exactly
in the image of God. When God created human beings
in His own image, why do human beings suffer? It's because human beings have forgotten their Creator; that's
why they suffer. Otherwise there is no difference between
man and God. The moment you realize that you don't
exist, but God exists, you are free. And in reality that's
true. All the scriptures say, God is omnipresent, omni-

scient, and omnipotent, God is everywhere. Then where are you? Where is there place for you to exist? How can you claim that you and I exist somewhere and this is mine and that is yours? It's the human mind that creates all the barriers for individuals. We have to understand this whole philosophy, get rid of all our confusions, be at peace and start realizing the great glory that is hidden deep within our hearts and minds. Therefore every individual should try to understand one thing: I will know myself on all levels in this lifetime and get enlightened here and now. There should be this determination. That is the purpose of this series of lectures.

What does the body mean to us? Is human being a body alone? No. He breathes too. Then you see we are breathing beings. This breath of ours creates a bridge between our thinking process, or mind, and body. Why does the body not fall apart, separating itself from the thinking portion? Because there are two guards, called inhalation and exhalation. Life is breath and breath is life.

How does our mind function and from where does our mind receive its power and energy? There is a center of consciousness beyond mind and that is called your individual soul. So it is from here that you receive consciousness and energy. Individual souls are like ripples in the vast ocean of bliss called Brahman, the summum bonum of life, the very source of all life force, from where all the ripples rise, play, and again subside.

Let's begin with the body. We take care of our body but do not understand anything about it. So if you want to be physically fit, understand the importance of a good body. Good body means, physically healthy body. You need to understand something about diet and nutrition, and about body language. Your body speaks to you.

When you learn to understand your body's needs and body language, then you should learn how to breathe. We all are breathing but we are not breathing correctly, not breathing diaphragmatically. You'll find that a child spontaneously breathes diaphragmatically but because of our defective living, our breathing changes after some time. So deep diaphragmatic breathing is very necessary for health (see Appendix A).

What is diaphragmatic breathing? When you push in your abdomen as you exhale, it will help your diaphragm to empty your lungs and will help you to expel the used up gas. When the abdomen moves out it will expand the lungs and draw in the oxygen.

It's easy to know the body and breath, but it's a little bit more difficult to know the mind, because there is no such education that teaches and trains us to understand our mind. So let us have simple understanding. Scientific research and scientists today say that 80% of diseases are created by the mind. They originate in the mind and are expressed in the body. All of the body is in the mind, but not all of the mind is in the body. You don't see your mind but through your mind your eyes can see. If you are frustrated all the time, never happy, then your wife says, "What can I do? He's never happy, no matter what I do. Very unhappy person, nobody can please him in this world. No matter what I do he's never happy." Poor husband is heading towards some problem!

As it is important for you to eat good nutritious food and to do some exercise daily, it is important for you to maintain mental health, spiritual health, by learning to do certain exercises of breathing, relaxation and meditation. It's very good for you. Once you have learned how to use your deep diaphragmatic movement to regulate the motion of your lungs, then you watch your breath stream. It's very joyous, wonderful. Who is giving you life breath? The Lord of life who gives to all. It's your direct link with the Lord that you have all the time. Watch your breath, the flow of breath and the mind will find an easy way to attain peace, to taste peace.

For a few minutes every day you should learn to sit quiet, to sit still, to make your breath serene, to make your mind calm. Practice will make you perfect, not mere theory. This is something that you have to practice. I cannot meditate for you. I can do anything for you; I can cook your meals, I can drive you from one place to another. But meditation is that something which you should practice yourself. Buddha clearly said, "Ye, light thy own lamp. Nobody can give you salvation." Meditation you should practice. A guru, a teacher, a priest, can give you blessings, and that gives you solace, good solace, but meditation practice you have to do yourself.

When you know you are not a body alone, that you are a thinking being, that you have a mind, then you ask, "Who am I? I have body and mind, who am I? Am I the body? No. Am I the mind? No. Then who am I?" You wonder. Then you don't identify yourself only with your body and mind. That which you are is called soul, hub of the whole wheel. How do you know that? Unless you make your body quiet, breath calm and mind completely resolved, you cannot reach your finest self. You are constantly identifying with the objects of your mind, forgetting your true nature. Your true nature is peace, happiness, and bliss. But you are suffering because you do not know yourself. You know only the small self called body, breath, and mind. You have three selves—mortal self, semi-mortal self, and the immortal Self. The mortal self is this body that goes through change, death, and decay.

Semi-mortal self is that which enables you to think. The real Self is that which makes you free, completely free. Then, there are no fears, there are no anxieties, there is no pain.

When you repeatedly do something, you form a habit pattern. What is individuality, what is an individual? An individual is a character composed of habit patterns. You say God created you the way you are. That's not true. God created you and you are beautiful. You are a most beautiful person. Don't look at the mirror to admire yourself. You are most beautiful because you are unique, there is no one like you on this earth. No one can be compared with you. So don't compare yourself with others. You are most beautiful, be aware of this. You are wonderful, be aware of this. God has created you in a wonderful way, try to learn this. So human beings have not attained the next step of civilization because of certain things, not because of God. If God comes down and says, "Ok son, what do you want from me?" What will you say, tell me? "I want to become a millionaire." "There are many millionaires." "I want to have two dozen cars." "There are many people with dozens of cars." What will you ask of God? What do you want from God? Finally you will say, "God, give me peace." God will say, "My child, I have given you all the potentials to attain peace." You can be at peace, you can make your mind tranquil and thus establish peace.

Our deeds, our karma, are the cause of all suffering. How can one live in the world, yet remain unaffected? First you have to understand the inevitable law of karma, which is a universal law, no matter from which community you come from. If you are a Hindu, you'll have to follow it. If you are a Christian, a Buddhist or of any other religion, you'll have to follow it. Never forget this universal law, accepted by all the great religions and bibles of the world: as you sow, so shall you reap.

I am doing my actions and I reap the fruits of my actions. And those fruits again motivate me to do actions and there is no end. It becomes a whirlpool. You all boast that you are doing your actions, duties, truthfully and you are right. But there is something missing in your statement. I once asked a housewife, a very gentle, very chaste, very loyal housewife, "Can you sit down for a few minutes?" She wanted to go home, but just to test her I said, "Just sit down for a second." She replied, "I would like to, but what to do? I have to do my duties." It means your duty has made you a slave. How to deal with it? You don't know how to handle it. So the great men say, learn to love your duty then duty will not make you a slave. A simple thing, grease your duty with love. Otherwise your duty will create bondage for you, you cannot live without doing your duty. If you have understood this key, then you will try your best to perform your actions and learn the philosophy of nonattachment which is called love. What we mistakenly call love is actually lust. Love means nonattachment. Love does not mean attachment. Attachment leads to misery and pain, nonattachment gives you freedom. As St. Bernard has said so beautifully, all the things of the world are to be enjoyed but God alone should be loved. Our scriptures also say this.

You have to make a formula if you really want to practice and enjoy life. I'm not telling you to renounce the world and go to the Himalayas with Swami Rama, this is not my point. I want you to live here and enjoy life and yet remain above, as a realized being, a *jivan mukta*. How is it possible? Many people become swamis and how many swamis disappoint us? I once asked my Master, "What is this fun in the world? So many swamis?" He said, "Look here, everybody has good intentions to do something but they don't. They are not competent, they are not able, they don't find the way, so don't blame anyone. They are trying, they are making efforts." I said, "Ok. Out of 13,000 swamis I met in my life, I met only three people, rare people." Then I said, "Why, why this?" He said, "All other swamis are like a hedge, and the rare ones are like the real flowers." He told me, "Come on. I'll make a formula for you. Share it with your students, share it with the people who come in touch with you: All the things of the world are meant for you. Please enjoy them. But they are not yours, don't get attached to them." You have no right to get attached to them. There is nothing wrong with your enjoyment. If there is anything wrong it's getting attached. Where are you committing a mistake? You get attached to the things of the world which are not yours. Actually they are meant for you. So the first principle is that all the things of the world are meant for me. I will enjoy them but I will not get attached. Second principle, I will be conscious of the truth or fact that the Lord of life is within me. Thirdly, I will meditate, go within, beyond body, breath, and mind, to enjoy that silence which is the living silence within. If you just follow these principles, you are free.

CHAPTER TWO

Four Primitive Fountains

The word stress has become a hot word today. We all talk about stress. Was there stress in ancient times too? There was, but it was called ignorance. Today stress means stress, we don't accept that it's part of ignorance. A human being is a citizen of two worlds, the world within and the world outside. He suffers because he has become an outsider. Those who are insiders do not suffer on account of this modern disease called stress. Times have changed. Nowadays, human life is governed by the economy. From morning till evening we do not know why we are rushing, where we are going, without any destination. The moment you become aware of yourself, understand something about yourself, you will really enjoy life. If you examine yourself, you'll see that you like to enjoy life in the external world on all levels — the five senses and the mind. Who's preventing you from doing so? Who gives you stress? Outsiders do not come to tell you to become stressed. What is the reason for stress? What is the cause of your suffering? You all are reactionaries. You do not have convictions. You may think about things, but you have not built an individual philosophy of life. I say, if you devote only ten minutes every day to yourself, you will not suffer on account of this stress.

The question is where does stress come from? Let us examine this. A human being cannot live without doing actions, it's not possible. And when he performs actions, he reaps the fruits of his actions and those fruits motivate him to perform more actions. This goes on and on, there is no end, and it becomes a whirlpool from which he cannot escape. When you examine your actions, you will find that your actions are commanded and controlled by your mind. If you do not think of doing something, you cannot do it. Your thought virtually is your action. Your thoughts, in turn, are controlled by your emotions. And from where do your emotions arise? They arise from four primitive fountains called food, sleep, sex, and self-preservation. We human beings are still primitive because *ahara, nidra, bhaya, maithunancha*, food, sleep, self-preservation and sex, still control human life exactly as they do in the animal kingdom. That is why they are called primitive fountains. You eat food, animals also eat food. You sleep, animals also sleep. You indulge in sex, animals also do so. You are afraid and all the time you are protecting yourself, as is the case with animals. You form a group, a particular group, animals also do the same. What is the difference between a human being and an animal?

There are four kingdoms: the kingdom of rocks, the kingdom of vegetables, the kingdom of animals, and the kingdom of human beings. In the process of evolution, a human being has attained the status of having choice, of being able to choose what he wants to do and avoiding that which he does not want to do. Self-control is found in the human kingdom, but an animal is controlled by nature, by the four fountains. Therefore, a human being has to take responsibility for his own deeds and actions. Definitely a superior being, he can communicate with others, narrate, discuss, talk and decide. So, by the creative use of emotions, a human can control his thoughts and hence, his actions. Emotional power is highest of all powers in a human being as far as the external world is concerned. And all emotions arise from the four primitive fountains. If these four fountains are properly understood, arranged and regulated, there will be no stress.

These fountains will help you in knowing and understanding your actions. You can find out the source of any problem that you have. You are angry today, and your children do not know why you are angry. You cannot beat your wife because you are afraid of her. You cannot beat your child because if you beat her, your wife, your whole family, even your neighborhood, will take you to task. So you take out your belt and start beating your dog. The source of your anger could be bad food. Bad food is that food which is not nutritious. Bad food is that food which agitates your nervous system. Bad food is that food for which there is no place in your body. Childhood training seems to be important here. A great musician is born in a musician's family. Why not outside? A great businessman is born in a businessman's family. We see how the environment affects the childhood and the child. Food has been a disaster for human health all over the world.

Food could be disastrous and yet no doctor asks you what kind of food you take. You go to the doctor and say, I have a pain here, but you didn't tell him why. What are your habit patterns, why do you have pain? There was a woman who had diabetes. Her husband said, "Honey, please don't take sugar." She replied, "I don't take sugar. Don't nag me." She was a Secretary in the Government of India, a highly placed person. He said, "I want your urine to be tested." Do you know what she did? Instead of sending a urine sample, she sent water. So Dr. Pandey, who was a famous pathologist, told me, "Look at this, Swamiji. What is this? She sent me water." He wrote, "Instead of sending urine, your wife sent water. Please ask her to send her urine before I examine her." She was surprised and wondered, "How can he know the difference between water and urine?"

So take care of your diet. Learn to eat that food which is right for you. If you clean your teeth properly, chew your food well, simple food which is healthy for you, which contains both liquid and solid, both vegetables and fruits, you will be healthy.

Once you have understood food, then you should understand deep sleep. Being able to sleep deeply is very healthy. Many of you daydream. Whole night you are going through the dreaming process. What is dream? Dream is an intermediate state between waking and sleeping. When you go from your living room to your bedroom, you go through a passageway, a gallery. Dream is the passageway between waking state and deep sleep. Though dream is therapeutic, it robs your sleep. If you go on dreaming, thinking that it's very therapeutic, you won't sleep. This way insomnia develops, and it is your own doing. You should go consciously to deep sleep.

What is deep sleep? You have not discovered it. You will not find books on the subject of sleep, about what sleep is. It's such a practical subject, but you don't find books on the anatomy of sleep. A human being conventionally sleeps for eight to ten hours. It is not needed. No creature, no human being, can sleep more than 2½ hours. Rest of the time he tosses and turns in his bed, half sleep and half dream. Because it's night, you feel you have to sleep. It's a myth. If you learn to sleep for 2½ hours, deep sleep, you will be rested. So you are deprived of sleep, you do not know why. You think when you are tired, then you should go to sleep. I say, do not do that. Sleep voluntarily. Make a determination, "I have to sleep 2½ hours and after that I have to wake up and do my duties, do my work. I have plenty of work to do." Why should we waste ten hours for sleep? What a waste of time and energy! Sleeping ten hours! Eating another three to four hours, fourteen hours? Look at the time we waste in dressing and just painting and polishing ourselves, becoming presentable. Another few hours spent in the bathroom. And what do you do with what's left of the day? Gossiping, talking to each other, about each other. What a waste of time!

So let me first tell you how to sleep and what sleep means to you. If you cannot sleep for some time, you cannot think right. In the morning you say, "I'm tired." When I look at you, you look tired and you have to use cosmetics to present yourself to others. It's not needed. You should be fresh in the morning if you have slept well. In the West, 75 million people are taking sleeping pills because they do not know the art of sleeping. And there is a way of sleeping that is called *yoga nidra*, how to sleep consciously and wake up on time. I observed many people like that. I went to Gandhiji's ashram with his son Ramdas who was the editor of the Times of India. And I saw Gandhiji sleeping exactly at the same time each night and waking up without any alarm. If you do not have a watch and your telephone is not working and if you have to go to the airport at five o'clock in the morning, you wake up before that. There is something in you which has got that power, that's called *sankalpa shakti*, the power of determination. So if you learn to sleep, you do not need more than 2½ hours, not at all. I myself cannot sleep more than 2½ hours and if I do, my body starts aching. I have to sit and do some work, either meditate, finish my ablutions, write a poem or make a sketch. I have to do something.

So first of all let me tell you not to waste eight to ten hours trying to sleep. According to the school of Buddhism, the greatest sin is not killing someone. No, no, no, greatest sin is called sloth, laziness. You cannot expect anything from a lazy husband. Housewives get upset because husbands are very lazy. I'll tell you one secret. The moment you wake up, immediately sit down. Don't remain inside the blanket, tossing and turning around, asking for a cup of tea. When tea comes, you say, "Hmmm, let me sleep some more." Train yourself. No one is going to help you in these areas. These subjects are not discussed in books or by teachers. All the teachers are repeating what they have heard, there is nothing practical. We know and know that we know, but we do not know how to practice, that is a serious problem. How to sleep? Before you fall sleep, for ten to fifteen minutes you should practise yoga nidra, voluntary sleep, how to sleep. If you learn how to sleep with the method of yoga nidra (see Appendix B) which has been examined and proven to be very useful, it will be very good for you. If you are tired after eight hours' work, then ten minutes' practice of yoga nidra will give you energy for another eight hours. This I have noticed. I don't claim anything unless it is based on scientific findings. And if you go on practicing, in a few days, sleep will be under your control, just like the way food is.

So I say, how much time do you waste when you sleep. If you are not sleeping well, if the quality of sleep is not good, you will have stress. And nothing can help you. Doctors can help you only so much. They can only cure a few diseases which are called infectious diseases, they cannot help you with 70-80% of diseases that are called psychosomatic diseases, created by your own mind. The whole world is sick and the sick are treating the sick. Hospitals are built by neurotics and psychotics live in them! And who collects the rent? Doctors. We are all groping in darkness. The time has come, awareness has expanded. Therefore we should learn the art of living, the art of joyful living. I have not seen a person who perennially smiles and claims, "I am happy in the world." Anyone you ask, says, "I have a problem." There is an art of sleeping, knowing how to sleep.

Sleep is a mystery. If a fool goes to sleep, he emerges a fool, nothing happens to him, there is no transformation. But if a fool goes to the deepest state of consciousness, he comes out as a sage. There is something beyond sleep. You have three states: waking, dreaming, and sleeping. Two people decided to visit a sage. They went over and they sat down beside him. One of them fell asleep and the other started conversing with the sage. One who started conversing was in *samadhi*, the other was asleep. It's very close, very close. You can take benefit of sleep provided you know what it is, how to sleep. It's an art. You sleep because your wife says, "It's ten o'clock now, switch off the lights." And you have come home with a catalogue of worries, a bundle of worries. You do not know what to do with those worries. But if you have a little bit of understanding, "Well, at night I cannot handle you, my worries. I can help you tomorrow morning, solve you tomorrow morning. This is the time for rest." If you start having a dialogue with yourself, you can help yourself. Before going to bed you should learn to breathe deeply. I am trying to give you a glimpse of that life which is a realistic, practical life.

One day I thought, "Let me experiment and see what happens when I'm falling asleep." And I could not sleep for many days. I wanted to watch how sleep comes. When there is no content in your mind, then you get sleep. Before you sleep, learn to breathe deeply, release from your system carbon dioxide, the used up gas, and inhale deeply. With this pleasant feeling go to sleep, and you can avoid nightmares. Don't just say, "relax, relax, relax, relax," and then try to sleep. Relaxation is not sleep. That's why the method of relaxation which includes breathing works on two aspects, two spheres, body and breath, food and *pranic* sheaths. And then mind has to relax. But if you suggest to yourself, "relax, relax, relax," this suggestion is hypnosis, not relaxation. And we are all hypnotized by ourselves everyday. And then you hypnotize your wife, and your wife hypnotizes you. You are under the spell of hypnosis all the time. And that's not a creative way of studying or a creative way of learning. So, when you understand the method of sleeping, "I have to sleep, I don't have much time. I have to get up, I have to teach, I have to write, I have to compose a poem, I have to make a painting. When do I have time?" With this determination, sankalpa shakti, you go to sleep and wake up exactly at the same time. I was taught that and it works with me. Those who know me closely know that I don't sleep at night. The best time of my life is at night when I can think, write, read, compose poems, do things. I'm not telling you to do this because your life is different.

You are laughing. In Germany, I was speaking in Hamburg before a huge crowd. I told a long joke, which took me a few minutes. And my interpreter, wonderful interpreter, translated it in such a way that everybody fell down from their chairs laughing. And just in few seconds' time! I thought, "I have wasted much time in learning English, Sanskrit and other languages. I am going to learn German." After the lecture was over, I asked her, "Tell me, how did you translate such a long joke in a few seconds' time?" She said, "I told them, look, the speaker is telling a long joke, so please laugh." One should maintain a sense of humor. You know, laughter is a good exercise. After taking your meals, you should learn to laugh. With your children, with your wife, laugh. Come on, with laughter, you remain very healthy. Sleep and food, if these primitive fountains are regulated, I tell you, you will enjoy good health. Your walk will be a dance, your life will be a poem, a song. The flower of humanity will bloom the day we understand these primitive fountains.

As sleep can be and should be regulated, you should also regulate another appetite called sex. It's an Eastern taboo. People don't discuss it. They think it's a sin to discuss sex. Parents do not know, either. They eagerly tell their children, "Now you are grown up, you should get married." They collect a good dowry and they look out for a good boy or a good girl. But they don't teach their children what marriage is, why they are getting married. So sex has remained a mystery throughout, "Oh, don't talk about sex, don't talk about it. It's vulgar." And the minds of many people are haunted by this primitive fountain all the time. You think about it, but you do not talk about it. And wife and husband, I have not seen them happy, pardon me, anywhere in the world, in the East or in the West. I traveled far and wide and asked them, "Are you happy?" "Hmmm, partial happiness." They lean on each other and they call it happiness. Wife needed someone, she was insecure, so she got a husband. Husband needed someone, a companion and he got a wife. There is no adjustment.

You talk about God. Tell me, from morning till evening, when do you need God? When you are hungry, you eat. When you are thirsty, you drink. Where do you get that idea, God, God, God? You do not deal with the issues which are directly related to your body, breath, senses, and mind. You waste your energy in thinking of things. So two people like to enjoy sex. Of course there is a joy that you derive through that union, physical union of man and woman and that's called *vishayananda*. But you cannot expand it. You have to keep repeating it. For a moment you feel joy, and then you remain sad the rest of the day. The momentary joy cannot be expanded forever and ever. That

vishayananda is not *paramananda*, or supreme joy. Therefore, where is that art of living in which two people know
how to enjoy the union, physical union? You cannot enjoy
because you don't have mental and physical control, you
don't. Let me tell you about a sociopsychological survey in
the United States, a very advanced country, an open country. The surveyers went to a nunnery and asked the highly
respected Mother Superior, "Ma'am, do you smoke?" She
said, "No, not at all." "Do you drink?" She said, "No." "Do
you have sex?" She said, "No." All the surveyors were surprised. She added, "But I have a small vice." "What is it?"
they asked eagerly. She replied, "I lie."

What is sex? What does sex mean to us? Now, a simple
point I am going to tell you. Men and women by nature are
created a little differently, biologically. And they should
learn to understand each other. If they do not understand
each other they can never be happy. Their whole life they
live together, depriving each other because of their ignorance of sex. You need to understand something about it.
What is this thing called sex which is so important? It is of
no use just shunning that particular aspect of life. One
should understand what it is. Why does it control my life?
Why have I been thinking of it all the time? What is it that
I cannot live without it, why? Why does a husband want to
go to another woman? Why are there so many divorces? In
the Western hemisphere, 50-60% of marriages end up as
divorces. Sex should be regulated. Man has got a different
mechanism than a woman. Biologically they are two different beings and they should understand each other. It is
a man's world, it has always been a man's world. Man has
never tried to understand woman. This is true, this is true.
She's like that horse who tastes the iron but the ironsmith
never tastes the iron, even though he works with iron his
whole life. Woman is a great power on this earth. If you

put a pebble on a man's tummy and tell him to walk for two hours, he cannot do that. A woman can carry a child for nine months without any difficulty. She goes through labor, it's like going through death. She goes through it pleasantly. If a man has a fever, oh my Lord, the whole neighborhood knows about it! Even biologically, you will find that there is a very low incidence of heart attacks among women, and many of these heart attacks are because of congenital defects. But man has heart attacks because he cannot tolerate stress, he has no shock absorbers. This field is totally unexploited because a woman has been used only for a particular purpose, "She should wait for me when I come home, inspire me." In my opinion, educational systems in the whole world need some modification. And children's education should be totally handed over to the mothers. One of the great poets says, "Give me the first seven years of my life, the rest you can take." But there is another poet who says, "A woman, a mother, should be trained twenty-two years before her marriage." A good mother will be responsible for creating good citizens and then we can expect a good society. That's why they need good care and respect, this is my point.

But what do you do with the natural urge, biological urge? Let us be realistic. You can ask a question, "What does a swami, a renunciate, do?" Yes, a swami is taught upward traveling. Best part of the initiation that is given to a real swami, from an authentic tradition, is that upward traveling where he enjoys without engaging in sex. When you release that semen you feel joy. A swami is taught, "Hey, if you feel joy when you release semen, think how much more joy you will experience by retaining it through upward traveling." Oh my Lord, this is a great joy. But it is an uncommon teaching. It cannot be made available for everyone to practice.

After understanding food, sleep, and sex, you should understand self-preservation. You want to preserve yourself, that's instinctual. Whenever there is a natural disaster, your pets know first, dogs know first, cats know first. Why do you not know? Because instinctual knowledge in you has diminished, mental knowledge has developed and your mind has limited capacity. It always tries to measure the whole universe with it's little ruler. There is another higher realm of knowledge that is called intuitive knowledge, which is beyond all the levels of your mind. So you are afraid all the time, "I will lose, I will lose, I will lose." Fears, many fears. All the time from morning till evening, you remain conscious of yourself and you remain protecting yourself, no matter what happens to others.

I have seen one aspect of life and that is maternal aspect. There is a place called Azamgarh in India, where in my early days I used to walk about barefoot. A wild elephant suddenly appeared in front of a mother who was walking holding her child's hand. When the elephant suddenly appeared, the mother pushed the child behind her and stood firm and said, "Stop there!" And you know, the elephant stopped. That demonstrates how great is a mother's love for her child, the greatest solace in life, a real symbol of love, though that's also changing now.

You remain conscious of yourself all the time, "What if something will happen to me, something will happen to me." Fear invites danger. You are afraid all the time, you are inviting danger, don't do that. I will tell you what happens. I was standing on the bank of the Ganges at Rishikesh when I was twenty-three or twenty-four years old. During those days I used to look towards the sun and move according to the sun the whole day. It is one of the practices. You don't do that, Ok? I did not know that there was a cobra beneath me. Sometimes I used to sit and then I would stand up. There was a swami watching from a distance and he shouted, "Swami, please don't move, there is a cobra beneath you." Naturally, I looked and saw the cobra. So, what did I do? I ran. And the cobra started chasing me, chased me up to fifty or sixty yards. I said, "I have never seen a cobra, a snake, chasing a human being like this." Then the swami told me, "Look, the cobra did not chase you, you were dragging it behind you. Your mind was so terrified, so afraid, that fear got concentrated and your negative mind dragged the cobra behind you." When you are afraid, you actually affect others. Fear invites danger, remember this. When you become negative, passive, and you are afraid, you invite danger for yourself. Don't get afraid for no reason. Don't remain under the pressure of fears.

Modern man is full of fears and he does not examine those fears. You should learn to sit down and examine your fears. What are my fears, what fears do I have? Nobody wants to examine their deepest fears. Sit down and try to examine what are the fears in my life. Will my husband desert me? Fear. Will my wife leave me? Fear. From morning till evening you are afraid of something. What kind of life is this? How can you enjoy life under the pressure of fears? So modern man wants to enjoy life, wants to have joyful life but he remains under the pressure of fears. He should learn to examine fears. Fear of not getting what he wants, fear of losing what he has. That does not allow you to enjoy life. Therefore, you should have understanding so that you don't entertain fears.

You have all heard about the former Prime Minister of India, Mrs. Indira Gandhi? A brave lady, not even afraid of bombs. I remember an incident with her. She was staying in a government guest house and I was staying in the next one. Suddenly at night she screamed. People thought that it might be the swami. So guards came and knocked on my door instead of hers and they found me seated in meditation. The Superintendent of Police said, "No, no, it's not him. Find out why she screamed." Who could ask the Prime Minister why she screamed? And she continued to scream. Finally the Superintendent of Police and the District Magistrate asked, "What can we do?" She shouted, "Open the door." They said, "It's locked from inside, ma'am." "Kick the door open." They kicked and broke down the door. There was a single spider going up the wall. She was not afraid of bombs, of bullets, but she was afraid of a small spider!

Sometimes we all have such fears. Fears that we don't discuss because we have created a mask around us. "How can I talk about my fears to my children, my husband, my friends? What will they think of me?" You keep the fears within you. That fear grows and grows and grows. I have gone through that. I was afraid of snakes. My Master knew this. So one day he said, "Come here, pick up these flowers." There was a heap of flowers and I picked them up. There was a snake in the heap. I said, "Snake, snake." He said, "So what?" He was in front of me and said, "I am here. I won't allow you to die." I said, "This is a black snake." He said, "Whether it is black or blue, bring it to me. You have to choose whether you respect your fear or you respect me." With great fear I walked up to him. He said, "Son, this creature is the cleanest in the world. There is no creature on earth which is cleaner. This is a most ancient creature on the earth, who lives on trees, who lives in the water, who lives on the land. Why are you doing this to yourself?" I said, "It bites and man dies." He said, "Human being is a greater snake than the snake itself." And the dialogue was going on, and I was holding the flowers and the snake. Finally he said, "Come on, touch it like this, but not that way." And that snake put up her hood and let me pet her. I said, "Sir, is it your tame snake or a wild one from the forest?" Thus my fear went away.

You should learn to examine your fears. Why are you committing the mistake of not examining your fears? Learn to examine your fears. A woman is afraid. If her husband is late from work, she will telephone the police station, the hospitals to find out what has happened to him. Why? Why think negatively all the time? Do you know what happens, what you are doing to yourself? Fear invites danger, remember this. Don't put yourself in danger.

From these four primitive fountains arise the streams of emotion. Your emotional problems are related to one of these four fountains, there is no fifth fountain. I am putting before you twenty-five years of experiments and studies. Somehow or other, all your fears, all your emotions are related to these fountains. Those emotions could be converted into creative emotions. Gauranga knew how to use emotion and attain a state of ecstasy. All the great men of the world, somehow or other came in touch with this, their emotional power. Wisdom through mind, through thinking, is not complete. Wisdom through emotion can lead you to heights of ecstasy. All the great sages following the path of bhakti or love, came in touch with this power.

So these four fountains, food, sleep, sex, and self-preservation, are related to each other closely, very closely. There was an Irish woman, whom I respected very much, I respected her like my mother. I never saw my biological mother in my life and so never missed her, but I really miss my Irish mother. She helped me establish the Himalayan Institute in the United States. Sometimes we used to fight with each other. At night she would quietly go to the refrigerator, eat, and in the morning swear that she had not eaten anything. I said, "Mama, it's not good." She said, "Son,

I promise I've not done anything, I've not eaten anything."
She would forget. When habit becomes deep-rooted, then
you give up. There is compensation, law of compensation.
She was not married, the psychological analysis was this.
And in an Irish family, they are very conservative and she
used to control all her brothers, their wives, children, and
everybody. She was the head of the family. And she did
not get married for the sake of the family. Remember this
formula, this point, all of the body is in the mind but all of
the mind is not in the body.

We talk of God, we talk of this bible and that bible,
we talk of this religion and that. It's of no use if we do not
understand the very basics in our life. Learn to regulate
these four fountains, because all your problems come from
one of these four. For example, you may be sexually frustrated and you don't speak of it to anybody, because the
customs, the culture, society does not allow you, does not
permit you to talk. And you go on bottling those ideas which
you cannot share with others. Then finally you become a
mental wreck, create psychosomatic problems for yourself.
Not only that, if you are eating bad food it can happen. If
you don't get sleep, if you don't understand how to sleep
deeply, you are not rested. In the state hospital I visited in
Kansas, I found everyone sleeping—eight hours, ten hours,
twelve hours, and relaxing. I fought with the doctors. What
you call relaxation is very dangerous. If you go on relaxing
your muscles, a time might come when the muscles will
lose their function. It's a simple, simple scientific law.

Sleep is a necessity of both body and mind, please
remember this. Food is a necessity of body first. Sex could
be a biological necessity, but actually it originates in the
mind. If it is not in the mind, you will not do sex. So you
should see, which is important, what is first prominent in
the mind and what is prominent for the body. Sex affects

mind first, then body. Food affects body first, then mind. Sleep affects mind first, then body.

You are the victim of your habit patterns. Who are you? You are the sum total of your habits, that's what you are. And your habits are the result of your repeated actions. Your actions, your deeds, are related to the four fountains. There are no books available for it. There are no books available on practical subjects anywhere, I tell you that. Self-discipline is missing in our educational life. Where are the teachers, the curriculum where children are asked to walk straight, to talk straight, to be gentle and straightforward? There is no such curriculum. These basic points are missing in our daily life. These disciplines should be introduced in the schools, they will be very helpful. Something about food, something about sleep, something about sex, something about self-preservation; these should be taught to our children. It will help them. We have to understand the primitive fountains if we want to lead a free, happy, joyous life.

CHAPTER THREE

The Body

World has nothing to offer you as far as enlightenment is concerned. But if you learn to arrange the world
around you, the world will not create barriers and obstacles
for you. If you keep on removing the obstacles, when will
you have time to realize? Learn to arrange your situation in
a way so that there are no obstacles and barriers created in
your family life, in your social life, in your financial life.
Then, you are free to meditate. Why do you want to learn
something about health? If you are very healthy, will it help
you to attain God? No. Then what good is health? A healthy
body will not create disturbance for you. It will not distract
you from your aim of attaining the purpose of life.

Your body speaks to you. The body has a simple and
subtle language. Nobody teaches you, but you have to learn
that language. If you overstrain, your body will tell you.
This consciousness will lead you to understanding, to self-
awareness, and then you will understand the capacity of
your body. Many things you do without understanding the
capacity of your body. This injures your body. You ignore
body language and what happens? Either you suffer on
account of malnutrition or you suffer on account of over-
eating. When you overeat, what happens to you? You start
burping. Body speaks to you. When you are tired what happens? Body starts aching. Body speaks to you but you don't

listen to your body. So first learn to understand your body language. This will keep you healthy.

If you have overslept, if you are lazy, you will feel dull. You do not do many things because of sloth, which is one of the greatest enemies of mankind. You talk about sins. But you know the greatest of all sins is sloth, laziness. You want to wake up at four o'clock. You have had complete rest, you have enjoyed the rest. But you are still trapped inside the blanket, tossing and turning, making some sounds but you do not get up. Laziness! The prime enemy of a human being is laziness. But once you understand the value of life, with currents and cross-currents, then you understand that there is no place for laziness in life. You can achieve tremendous things in this lifetime. Look, one-fourth of your life is spent in eating, a fourth goes in sleeping, another fourth in the bathroom, and the remaining fourth in dressing, talking about others, condemning and praising others. Is this life? Tell me, what will you gain?

From the viewpoint of both yoga and Ayurveda, there are two systems functioning in your body. One system is busy cleansing this city of life called the body. Another system is constantly nourishing this human life. Your pores, lungs, kidneys, and bowels, are busy cleansing the city of life. Your heart, brain, spleen and liver are nourishing the body. There is coordination established between these two systems in your human life. They are functioning well together.

To maintain a healthy body you need to first understand something about diet and nutrition. Secondly you should have some knowledge of liquids. Vegetables are nourishing, fruits are cleansing, have a cleansing effect. Your diet should have both. Your diet, no matter whether you are a vegetarian or nonvegetarian, should have enough vegetables, because the latest research conducted in universities and scientific laboratories all over the world says that too much meat-eating might lead to cancer of the colon.

Being a vegetarian or a nonvegetarian depends upon your culture, tradition and country. I have seen that Eskimos are good meditators, even though they have nothing else to eat but meat. In that climate, in those conditions, they have no other alternative but they are still good meditators. I do not want to enter into a controversy about this. I'm a vegetarian because in the Himalayas you don't get much meat. So from the very beginning I was brought up with vegetables. If I bury vegetables in the ground, I can grow vegetables. But if I bury a piece of meat, it will create only germs. The greatest, the biggest and wisest of all animals, the elephant, is a vegetarian. The tiger is very fast and rash, but it cannot fight for more than two hours. Therefore, I personally prefer to be vegetarian but I don't tell people that they should be vegetarian. This, I don't. If you can afford and accept vegetarianism, it's good, but don't prepare for divorce because your wife is not accepting vegetarianism and you want to. She may eat the meat of a goat, and the goat eats grass, so she can be called a secondary vegetarian!

Learn to eat good food, food which helps you maintain good health. Your food should be cooked but not overcooked. Many people become fanatical and ask why food should be cooked. Well, your intestines are not meant to digest raw food. That's why food should either be steamed or baked, but not overcooked to the point that the food value is destroyed. When you overcook food what happens? The natural calciums turn into inorganic calciums for which you have no place in your body. Take fruit juice. If you go on heating juice, overheat the juice, then all the germs of the juice will die. The nature of the juice will change. If you do not know how to extract the juice, if the fibers are not properly squeezed, then all the nutrients are left behind in the fibers. What good is that juice? Some understanding, some study, some research should be conducted on the food that you eat, that's my point.

What we give to our children is food plus poison. Mothers cook food that is tasty, that is pleasant to the palate. Children like such food but that food is not healthy for their bodies. Too much roasting and toasting of food is not healthy. It could be very tasty, but it has no nutrition, no nutrients. Therefore, you have to be food conscious. That will train your children, the coming generation. I am not giving you a sermon. I am imparting some practical knowledge to you.

Simple food is healthy food. Do you really taste the food? No. You taste only the *masalas*, the spices. Too much of spicy and greasy food is very unhealthy. Please, my daughters, no greasy food. Why don't I accept your invitations for lunch? It's because of this reason, because I lead a health-oriented life. Learn to cook meals which are not greasy, and you will be healthy. You will be doing a great favor, a service to your husband and children. Many Indian mothers think that *ghee*, clarified butter, has some special value. We have done many experiments. Ghee has nothing, no vitamins. It is a very good cooking medium but please don't overuse it. It's especially injurious to your heart. It can create CHD, coronary heart disease. If you take too much ghee, then you have to work hard to digest it. Those who work in the fields, those who are in the army, they can use ghee and sugar, others should not. They are very injurious.

I tell you something, no matter where Indians, Japanese, Chinese, Southeastern Asians, go, they eat greasy food. And they consume at least 120 pounds of sugar every year. I am talking of research conducted honestly. You should understand that anything that you eat is converted to sugar by your body. The body creates sugar, builds sugar. That creates another 120 pounds sugar. So 240 pounds sugar per year! Oh my Lord, what poison! You cannot eat food without sugar? Why? Why do you want to eat extra sugar? This creates imbalance in your body, disturbs your metabolism and the functioning of your pancreas. Look at the salt you consume. You don't need that much salt. So if you can change your dietary habits by avoiding too much roasting and toasting the food, killing the food, too much grease, extra sugar and salt, then you will not suffer on account of many, many diseases.

One thing I want to warn Indian women, a very bad tradition we have. Our food habits are disastrous. There was a German writer who lived in India for twenty-five years and spoke many Indian languages: Malayalam, Tamil, Telugu, Hindi, Gujarati, Urdu, Bengali, Punjabi, many languages. He studied Indian food and he lived with Indian families. And he wrote, "An Indian woman, my Lord, is the best in the world. Only she can live with a stupid Indian husband." Sorry, I am not saying it, that's what he wrote! A conventional Indian husband is sitting down and water is next to him but he calls out to his wife who runs out from the kitchen, asking, "What do you want?" "Give me water," he says even though the water is next to him. Then the German writes, "An Indian woman is wonderful. There is no woman on earth who can be compared with an Indian woman as far as home life is concerned, but there is one thing, she's very dangerous! She's a murderess." I said, what's this? I was shocked to read this. He writes, *kehti hai*, *"Thodasa aur khalo, aur khalo, aur khalo."* She says, "Please eat a little more, a little more, a little more." She wants to please her husband and so the whole day she spends in the kitchen. An Indian wife overfeeds her husband. He gets fat, has high cholesterol, high blood pressure, diabetes. And finally he has a heart attack and she becomes a widow. He writes, "India is full of widows going to the temple and crying, remembering their husbands." Preventive medicine is an important part of modern life. Why should we be sick? We should be aware of health, we should be aware of diet and nutrition, we should be aware of good living, of how to eat right.

Now let us look at experiments that we have done. A child was given chocolates all the time. And another child was trained not to give chocolates, not to take chocolates. The child who took chocolates, sweets and sugar all the time was cranky, used to cry and was angry all the time. Even my typist, Theresa King, who is a writer, had rashes all over the body. She went all over the world but nobody could heal her. She went to skin specialists in France, Germany, England, America, many places. So one day she was typing with her whole body covered with rashes and she asked, "Can't you help me, Swamiji? I have spent more than $300,000." I said, "You never asked me." I said, "In five minutes time, you can be cured." She said, "Five minutes? Well, I have been helping you, why are you not helping me?" I said, "Stop eating chocolates and in one week you will be cured completely." She used to eat chocolates all the time. And I gave her the upper wash and the full wash the next day and I reminded her, "Now, no more chocolates." Her husband told me that even in her dreams, she used to say, "Oh Lord, oh chocolate, oh chocolate, oh chocolate." In a week's time she was completely cured. She completely stopped taking sugar. Look at the change. Now she goes to everyone and says, "Do you take sugar?" If someone says, "Yes," then Theresa tells them, "You are not my friend."

There are many such diseases that the doctors cannot

figure out because you are not telling them about your habits. Most of the diseases, at least 80% of the diseases, are self-created, because of our not understanding simple ways of life. Balance, balance, balance. Simple food, nutritious food, fresh food, that helps you. To enjoy good health is very beneficial for you.

Many of you are anxious to know how to lose weight, aren't you? I will tell you a simple method. But I know you are not going to do it. Eat whatever you want to, but eat the way I want you to eat. You do not chew your food well. If you go on chewing your food well, you cannot overeat, let me tell you this. You'll find an improvement in your digestion. Count thirty-six and chew, you cannot overeat. You overeat because you don't relish food, you just fill up the belly and it expands. Filling up your tummy, converting it into a pantry, is not good for you, is unhealthy for you. You are not paying attention to your meal, you are not tasting the food. You actually live to eat, yet you don't have time to eat. What a horrible thing.

You are trained to do things in the external world. I will tell you to do something that is very delightful. Now those who have bad digestion, they should try this. In all great traditions, when you sit at the dining table, there is something called saying grace. Remember God before you eat. Do you know why it is done? Do you mean to say that God comes down to eat your food? It has a scientific purpose. You are calming down and giving enough time for saliva and other gastric juices to flow in readiness to digest the food. That's the point. You have to calm down. If you are angry, let me assure you, your endocrine system will not secrete well. Your tongue will become dry and there will be imbalance in your saliva and gastric juices.

Wife and husband should not make the dining table into a fighting ring. Husband is very busy, he has no time.

And wife waits the whole day and she gets frustrated. He's tired and has many, many preoccupations. He has no time, he doesn't want to discuss anything. And she wants to discuss. And there is only one time and that is at the dining table. It's unhealthy to fight at the dining table. You can fight, it's therapeutic. Not to fight may be injurious. But to make the dining table into a fighting ring is not good. It's therapy to let out your steam in a nice way. To bottle up is not good. So sometimes you swear, let out your steam on each other, that can be therapeutic, it's Ok. But there are two times of the day when you should learn to be calm. Please listen to me. I am talking on the basis of the scientific experiments we have conducted. Wife and husband should have this understanding, "We will not fight before we eat. We will not fight just before we go to bed. Honey, if you want to fight, you can fight before going to bed, but not while going to bed." That should be the understanding. Fighting at these two times directly affects the biological part of our life. It disturbs you. You fight and then you notice that your digestion is disturbed, your sleep is disturbed. Those homes where there is culture are homes where they calm down first, say grace and then eat their food.

The dirtiest part of your body is your mouth. You can injure people by saying something bad. If you shoot somebody, that hurt can be healed. But if you say something bad to your wife or to your husband, perhaps he or she might forgive you but will never forget. It happens. So do not hurt, harm or injure anyone through your speech. Besides bad speech, another dirty aspect of the mouth is your teeth. If your teeth are not cleaned properly, your liver will never remain healthy. Very few people know this, even the dentists do not know how to clean their teeth. It's shocking to me because I'm a scientist, I observe. Therefore, you should learn to regularly clean your teeth.

When you eat your food, chew your food well in a state of calm and quietness. Don't get frustrated, don't get angry at your husband, then overeat without understanding what you are eating. And then you get fat and he says that you have become very fat. Don't give him that chance. Don't let him become lazy. Kick him on his bottom if he doesn't exercise. You have every right to do that. If your husband doesn't exercise, be strong, tell him he has to exercise. You should learn to help each other, that is called partnership. You shouldn't destroy each other.

Understanding and simple prevention can help you stay healthy. We have come to know that in women, many cases of cancer of the cervix, more than 60%, occur because of lack of understanding of simple hygienic principles. The Tata Research Institute found that 50% of these cancers decreased after the women were taught how to clean themselves. Those who chew tobacco, who sniff tobacco, or who smoke excessively, suffer on account of cancer of the tongue. Certain types of diseases can be controlled, that's my point.

I don't understand what fever is. When you talk about cold and cough, I understand. But when you talk about fever, I fail to understand. This is because I have never had fever in my life. Why? I can create temperatures of more than 114 degrees in my body. No one has recorded anywhere in the world, a fever of over 108 degrees. You have so much potential, you can prevent many illnesses, this is my point. Don't give up and say I need a pill, I need a doctor, I need my psychologist. Don't remain like this all the time. You have many, many potentials and when you understand yourself, you'll find that there is a great doctor sitting within you. Cheerfulness is the greatest of all physicians. Learn to be cheerful all the time.

Another habit you have to form is to exercise regularly. There are some exercises which we teach, that are called emergency exercises. Yes. This world has become a world of economy. Do you know economy reading? Today, people buy a book but they don't have time to read. They only read the introduction and that is called book reading. So you should learn to do this unique exercise in the morning, *agni sara* (see Appendix C), which activates your solar system. If someone does that exercise regularly, he will be very healthy.

What is the human body? These arms, and legs and feet, they are not considered to be the human body. They are called upper and lower extremities. Your human body is only between the base of the spine and the top of the head. Now when you sit, sit with the head, neck, and trunk in a straight line. That's all. What should be your posture? When you talk of posture, posture does not mean twisting your legs and going to the doctor the next day. Keeping your head, neck, and trunk in a straight line is called posture. Learning to sit. Now here, when you talk about posture, if you go deeply, you'll come to know, no matter how many postures you do, you are not yet a yogi. Many people pay attention towards posture and they think that by standing on the head they become great yogis. No. Standing on the head really means learning to stand on your own feet. And if you have not learned that, what good is that? So no matter which posture you sit in, keep your head, neck, and trunk in a straight line and assimilate your upper and lower extremities in such a way that they do not disturb you. That's the importance of posture. You should practice for a few days that which is a comfortable posture for you. During meditation keep head, neck, and trunk straight and aligned. That's the first thing you should learn.

Now please let me explain. What am I doing? I am keeping head, neck, and trunk in a straight line. This is head, this is neck, and this is trunk. Along your spinal column lie three ganglionated cords, sympathetic and parasympathetic systems. In the center is centralis canalis and on both sides two ganglionated cords. I am giving you a very important lesson, please. I have seen you walking, all of you. How do you walk? You are walking hunched up like this. A young man walks like an old man. What is this? And if you walk like this, that is not a healthy walk. Even if you walk fast, you don't keep your head, neck, and trunk in a straight line. Now, if you walk hunched up like this, you are not allowing energy to flow from pelvis to medulla oblongata. If you do not keep your spinal column straight and walk like this or sit like this, you are punishing yourself. If you keep your spinal cord straight and then walk, you can walk for many miles and yet you will be not tired, because you are not putting weight on your locomotors. Always remember that if you want to become old early, then walk hunched up. If you want to remain young forever then walk straight. It's one of the secrets, I tell you. Walk straight, and enjoy your walk like a dance. When you walk, you are walking like it's a dance, you are walking like a tiger. In fifteen to twenty days' time, you will form the habit of keeping your head, neck, and trunk in a straight line. That will be very pleasant. That's very good for your health.

After understanding the four primitive fountains, understanding diet, nutrition and posture, then you have to learn something that you have not done before, that will benefit you. Learning to sit still, not doing anything, just making your body still. Whenever you try to discipline anyone, even a child, they become rebellious. Body becomes rebellious. First few days your body will rebel for lack of practice but in one months' time, your body will become still and you will find a great joy, a joy which you cannot find elsewhere. I tell you friends, you are missing something. All your joys are haunted by your fears. Learn to have inner strength so that you enjoy things in the world. *Veerabhogya vasundhara.* Only the brave can enjoy the things of the world, not the weak. Learn to sit still for a few minutes, five minutes will help you. There is no other method of giving rest to your involuntary system, let me tell you that. There is no medicine, there is no method except this, how to be still. It is a simple method, how to be still. If you keep the mind busy, lead the mind through a system, it will help your mind. And you should have a little taste of that practice. I will lead you to that. A few minutes of learning to be still, watching all the parts of your body systematically, from head to toe, learning to relax. Relaxation is not sleep, remember that. Don't sleep during relaxation. Survey your whole body from head to toe, relaxing every part of your body. Your mind has the capacity to do that. Your mind can locate the tension points, the stresses in your body. Stress can occur through your muscles too. Stress of muscles is different, stress of your nervous system is different, stress of your mind is different. But mind is the commander of your body and nervous system, therefore mind should be trained not to have any stress in your body. After a few days you will find that the body has become still. Learning to be still is called journey without movement, a unique journey.

Having learnt to be still, gently close your eyes. If you keep your eyes open, they will distract you. Gently close your eyes. Pay attention that your body does not move. Now, what happens, body will move. Body will create many gestures because it has never been disciplined. Many fools think that they have now awakened their *kundalini*, the divine power. They have not, it is only body disturbance. After a few days, a month, you'll find your body very still and calm. Then there are subtle disturbances, which are called twitching. In two months you will be able to make body very still and you will experience a kind of joy that you have never, never experienced in anything of this world. This is a secret that I'm revealing to you.

Don't practice for more than ten minutes, please don't. Because you don't have the capacity, you'll start thinking and hallucinating, so don't do it. Ten minutes stillness without any turmoil and twitchings and jerks, will give you immense joy. You immediately jump, you have not trained your body, you close your eyes and start hallucinating. You are cheating your wife and children. Yeah, you are escaping. As you are not earning enough, your wife might nag you, so you sit in meditation. Many husbands do like that. They cannot handle the situation at home, so they become meditators and say, "I am Swami Rama's disciple." I say, "No, you are not." And the wife telephones, "Hey rascal swami, what are you teaching my husband?" I replied, "Look, I have not taught him anything." I have faced these problems, I'm telling you. Don't use meditation as an escape. First few days you should learn. I will give you six months. In six months' time you can attain that which one cannot attain even after many, many years. And my method is not mingled with any religion, excuse me. It is purely scientific, based on experiments done in many laboratories of the West, and taken from the most ancient scriptures and approved by the great sages. So I am not teaching you anything that I do not do myself. I have not come here to make a platoon of fools, no!

CHAPTER FOUR

The Breath

We are all breathing the same air. There is only one proprietor of all who is supplying life breath to us. Who is giving you this life breath? The Lord of life, who gives it to all. Breath is a direct link with the Lord that you have every day. It's a perfect philosophy. Besides the philosophical aspect, it is also a practical science that is known to only a fortunate few. Your breath is like a barometer that registers both your mental conditions and physical conditions. Breath is the bridge between the body and your thinking process called mind. In our modern world, we either talk only about the body or about the mind but we have not done much research on the breath. The science of breath is a science unto itself. From the age of three, I have been doing experiments on breath. I have done experiments not only in the traditional monasteries of the Himalayas but also in modern laboratories all over the world. I am talking to you based on this experience and not merely because I have read something somewhere. In ancient scriptures, yogis who do research on the breath are called *prana vedins*. They can suspend their breath for a long time, even for months and months. You don't have to go so deep.

What is your body? That something which you can touch, grab, understand is called your body. Your body is

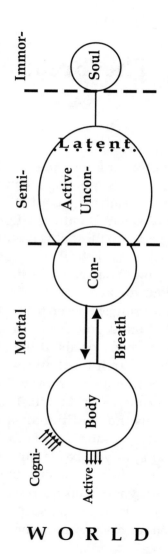

Figure 1

composed of five gross elements: earth, water, fire, air, and space. It's like a jar. You break the jar, earth goes to earth, water goes to water, fire goes to fire, all the elements go to their respective elements. It's a very interesting subject. Look at *Figure 1*. You are not body alone. Now this body is related to your thinking being. Who connects you with your thinking being? This is not discussed in books. No book explains why your thinking and physical being function together. I have not seen any book like that. So this is your thinking self and this is your physical self. How do the thinking self and physical self function together? There is a link between the two and that is called *prana* in Sanskrit. In English we call it breath. Life is breath and breath is life. This breath of ours creates a bridge between our thinking process and body. Please pay attention to this diagram, it will help you. Our thinking process is divided into two compartments, the conscious mind and the unconscious mind. There are two guards constantly guarding the city of life and they are called inhalation and exhalation. This is such an important link, but see what the scientists are doing. They talk of body, food, vitamins, exercises; they talk of mind and its analysis; but then nobody talks about the breath, because no one knows. Very few experiments are being done. For pregnant women, they have some breathing exercises. Otherwise no one knows much about breath. "We are all breathing," they say, "what is there to be learnt?" I say you are breathing, but you are not breathing properly, you are not breathing accurately. There are five main pranas and five secondary pranas in your body. Some of them supply energy to your body and there are others that cleanse your body.

Let us explain this diagram and understand life with it's currents and cross-currents, with all it's values. What does the body mean to us? Is the human being a body alone? No. He breathes too. Body without breath has no value, and if we have a body and breath but if there is no thinking, then that human being is also of no use. And if there is a human being who thinks, who breathes and whose body functions, that is also meaningless if he does not direct all his energies, mind, action and speech according to the purpose of life. Inhalation and exhalation are constantly guarding the city of life. Inhalation will become impossible if you do not exhale. Exhalation will become impossible if you do not inhale. If you take proper care of the cleansing systems of your body, your pores, lungs, kidneys and bowels, then the nourishing systems of the body will also remain active. That is why yoga manuals talk about certain *kriyas*, cleansing methods for your body. These are simple techniques, please do not make things complicated. If somebody says catch hold of your nose, do it directly, don't go around your head.

Once we have understanding about the body, diet and nutrition, then we have to know how to breathe. We all are breathing but we are not breathing correctly, that's why we suffer. Diaphragmatic breathing—how healthy it is. If you do not do diaphragmatic breathing, no *pranayama* can be learned by you. The teachers cannot teach you properly. Many teachers do not understand the importance of deep diaphragmatic breathing and they teach many methods of pranayama and these won't help. Deep diaphragmatic breathing is primary, something basic, that will help you prepare for pranayama, for higher methods of breathing exercises. Now watch the movement of your abdomen as you breathe. When you push in your abdomen it will help your diaphragm, the healthiest muscle in your body, to push in your lungs which will help you to exhale completely, expelling carbon dioxide. When the abdomen moves outward, it will expand the

lungs and create more space for the oxygen. Deep diaphragmatic breathing is very good for your health.

Having learnt to breathe diaphragmatically, you
should become aware of four bad habits of breathing. Four
no's. One is, no noise in the breath; two, no shallowness;
three, no jerkiness; and fourth, no pause between inhalation and exhalation. Now most of the heart attacks in the
world are because of bad breathing. There are other reasons too, but this is one of the primary reasons. I tell you,
no cardiologist can challenge me on this. Animals who
breathe shallowly do not live for a long time. A yogi does
not live the way others live. He lives according to the breath
he takes. You can expand your life if you understand this
science. Your breath should be deep without any sound.
It should not be heavy breathing. Sometimes people snore
and you can hear them even in the next building. Jerky
breath is also not good for you. Between inhalation and
exhalation and also between exhalation and the next inhalation, you create a momentary pause. Pause means
death. If I inhale and never exhale, what will happen? I
am dead. And if I exhale and then I never inhale, then
what will happen? I am dead. Death means pause between inhalation and exhalation. Unconsciously you are
creating a pause. Have you seen what children do sometimes? They don't exhale for some time and they faint. In
murcha pranayama, we teach our students to have control
over the pause. Don't allow that pause to be increased.
Pause is a killer. A human being is constantly killing many,
many tissues of his brain all the time. There are more than
10 billion cells in your brain. And many of these cells are
dying all the time. Why? Because of the pause. If that pause
expands, we die. Through proper breathing, you can remain healthy. You can maintain your health with simple
things. You can protect yourself from many diseases by

these preventive methods. You can live for a long time, which you want to, and enjoy the world. But you should have the capacity, you should have strength. And that strength should be inner strength, strength from within.

So when you understand something about these two guards of inhalation and exhalation, you understand a lot about life. In yoga manuals there are three phases of breath mentioned, inhalation, *puraka*, exhalation, *rechaka*, and controlled retention or *kumbhaka*. Pause means kumbhaka. It should be controlled, it should be under your control. Anyone who has controlled the pause is victorious and he is free from the call of death. He has controlled death. That's how yogis do it. That is pranayama.

Breath is related to your thinking process and to your body, it's a link. Who's responsible for maintaining the link? Why do they not fall apart? When you are thinking of going to your office, why do you not go to somebody else's office? When you are thinking of going home why do you not go to somebody else's home? What is that coordination between the thinking portion of your self and body? Tell me. Your breath is the bridge between the two, and as long as this breath is intact, you are living. The moment they fall apart it is called death. Separation of this thinking process and body is called death. So as long as we are breathing, these units function together. The moment these two guards cease functioning, separation occurs. What is separation? Death. What is unity? Life. Death is a habit of the body, a deep-rooted habit of the body. You are afraid of it, you don't want to think about it. "Oh, don't talk about it, don't think about it." You threaten a child that if he cries, the ghost will come and take him away. So it's the ghost of ignorance that haunts your minds all the time. Once you know what death is, it will not scare you. So now you understand, death means separation, unity means life.

Death does not mean complete annihilation. You live even after death. Yes, your body and conscious mind are separated from your unconscious mind and soul. Your body, breath and conscious mind that function during the waking state constitute your mortal self. The combination of unconscious mind and individual soul is semi-immortal. The individual soul by itself is immortal. When individual soul and unconscious mind separate from the conscious mind, breath, and body, that separation is called death. Here we find a clear definition of death. After one dies, he or she still exists. Many people think that death will free them from all their anxieties, all their problems. Forget it. It's not possible. It's just like falling asleep. If you sleep eight hours, how is this going to solve your financial problems? A long night's sleep is called death. It is never going to solve anyone's problems. Don't wait for death. Life's problems are never solved by death. They should be solved in the living state by us and that can be done here and now.

Wives will often say that their husbands are breathing horribly. How are they breathing? A long inhalation with a short exhalation or a long exhalation with a short inhalation. What is happening to you? This disturbs the motion of the lungs. The lungs are like a fly wheel in the machine called body. All night long, because the lungs of this great machine are disturbed, the right vagus nerve is disturbed, so the pumping station or heart is disturbed and therefore, brain is disturbed. How can you sleep? You can never have a good memory if you breathe like this. Simple thing is, not to allow a long pause. *Prana apana gatirudhva pranayama parayana.* Prana and *apana*, inhalation and exhalation, can be controlled very easily. So your sleep is not a good quality sleep, you cannot get rest. What type of rest have you been taking? That's why in the morning you are not rested. Even eight hours', ten hours' sleep, you look as though somebody has beaten you up very badly. Rest should give you freshness of face.

When sleep cannot give total rest, conscious rest is important. Five to ten minutes in the morning and five to ten minutes in the evening you should learn to give rest to yourself through meditation, a simple method. Learn to sit still. If you are not accustomed to sitting cross-legged on the floor, you can sit in this posture called *maitreyi asana* in the Buddhist scriptures. Place your hands on your knees, close your eyes gently and breathe.

Breathe deeply and diaphragmatically without noise, jerks or pause. Then watch the stream of your breath. You don't have to search for any other object to concentrate upon. As you watch the flow of your breath, your mind will find it easy to attain, to taste peace. You know what peace is? Peace is a gap between two wars. This peace that you taste is a gap between two thoughts. A thought comes and you get rid of that thought. There is a moment when another thought has not yet come. That period is called peace. If you can expand that moment which is between two thoughts, that is called meditation.

What to do next? I am giving this lesson now for the advanced students. After you have learned how to sit still, after you have learned how to have serene breath, after you have learned how to concentrate on the breath, you'll find that one of the nostrils remains blocked, that is, less open than the other. Rarely will you find that both nostrils are flowing freely. The activation of the left nostril is called *ida* and that of the right is called *pingala* in the yoga manuals. Ida is the moon and pingala the sun, night and day. When the day weds the night, at dawn, there is *sandhya* or joining of night and day. Similarly, at dusk is the sandhya of day and night. These are the best times for meditation because at these times both nostrils will flow freely, with sandhya between ida and pingala. This sandhya is called application of *sushumna* (see Appendix D). For sushumna application, learn to concentrate on the space between the two nostrils. Slowly you'll find both nostrils are flowing freely. When both nostrils start flowing freely, during that time you can never think of anything bad. During this sandhya of the two nostrils you should learn to meditate and you will experience joy, which the *rishis*, the ancient sages say is the joy of sushumna. This means you should learn to create a situation for your mind to be joyous if you want to meditate.

You can learn how to breathe before you go to bed, before you eat, and in the morning. Three times a day, five minutes at a time it will help you. Deep, easy breathing which does not need much effort. You want to eat the best food but you do not want to breathe properly? That's not healthy. The moment you wake up, just sit down and make your body still. Now, if a fool eats, he comes out of the dining hall still a fool. If a fool engages in sex, he comes out from his bedroom still a fool. If he sleeps, he wakes up as a fool. But if he goes to meditation he'll come out as a sage. How to meditate? First step is to be still, then next step is to breathe harmoniously and the third step is to let go.

Now let me tell you something. Your mind and your breath are two great friends, inseparable friends, they work together. Therefore when you train your breath, your mind is being trained, for they live together, they are very close friends. To bring the mind under your conscious control means to train your breath which you can easily do. You can easily control that mind which is called roving mind, and once you are able to do that, you'll have faith in your practices, you'll have confidence and then you'll go beyond. For that, a little bit more effort is required, but nothing is impossible.

CHAPTER FIVE

The Mind

I have not come to teach you religion for that you already have. I have come to teach you something that you do not have, that which is missing. And that's called a personal philosophy of life, which will support you no matter where you go. So I will tell you something about the mind and what is beyond the mind. I would like to give you both views, eastern and western, and try to explain to you the various aspects of mind and its modifications, so that there is no confusion and you can start working with yourself. We human beings are fully equipped and we can all attain the goal of life here and now. But sloth or laziness is the greatest of all sins. You have to work hard to learn anything. To learn English I had to work hard. Without working hard how can you accomplish anything? You have to know the language first, then you have to know the practice and finally, you have to follow it.

If you want to work with yourself you should start practicing and watch your activities and not be trapped by self-created misery that rises out of sloth. The question is have you decided? Are you determined to work with yourself? How long will it take? Ten minutes a day to work with yourself. In the external world you can get lost easily, but within, there is no chance of getting lost. Why are you afraid? Afraid of whom? Actually, all the fears are

within you, are created by you, all the fears are yours.
You have never examined them, that is why you are suffering. Therefore, O human being, learn to work with yourself. East and West meet here, and a day will finally come
when all of humanity will say with one voice that the mind
is the source of all problems and the mind is the source of
all pleasures. They have been trying their best to explore
something they do not understand. And this is true.

Whenever you sit down and examine your mind there
is some image in your mind. Image within is called imagi-
nation. And you are brooding on that image and when
that image passes, another image comes. Often, this is how
we think, "Who does my neighbour think she is? She
thinks that she has plenty of money. She thinks that she is
better dressed than I am, that she has bigger diamonds
than me. Who does she think she is?" All the time you go
on thinking this way and waste your time and energy.
Thus, the purpose of human life is defeated, because no
one teaches you how to use this brief span of life such that
life becomes productive, creative and fulfilling. But there
is a way. This brief span of life can be utilized, and in this
lifetime itself one can attain the purpose of life, one can
become self-realized.

Many of us think that the mind cannot be tamed,
cannot be polished, cannot be used, cannot be made useful. This is not true. Some of the great men have done it.
Many of us want to, but we don't practice. We have to
understand something about the mind. You can easily understand the mind by understanding your thought patterns. A thought comes, then another thought comes, then
another, another, another and this keeps on going. If you
study your brain wave patterns you will find that there is
a space between two thoughts. If you can eliminate this

space between thoughts, there will be only one thought.

Cleansing the mind, purifying the mind, means learning to train it, just like training or breaking in a shoe. If you learn to train your attention, you can do wonders in the world. In tropical countries, the temperature often goes above 130 degrees, but you cannot cook your meal with that heat because it is not concentrated. Somewhere else the temperature goes down very low. You cannot run your air conditioners with that. What you need is a concentrated source. Similarly, if you train your mind so as to be able to concentrate well, you can transform your whole personality. Even if you cannot change anything in the world, you can transform your life and you can do wonders in your life. There are simple methods to achieve this. We, who are considered to be teachers, have made things very complicated. If they put it simply, perhaps it will be very simple to understand. Also they drag the students towards themselves. I think the subject should be followed, not the teacher. Teacher means knowledge, knowledge should be followed. The individuality should not be given much importance; the subject should be given much more importance. Yoga science suffers on account of this. One teacher says, "This is the right method." Another teacher says, "No, only my method is the right one." The poor student is confused. After some time he finds his mind is robbed, his individuality is robbed, his pocket is robbed.

Things are very simple if you learn to be practical. What does being practical mean? Practical means that anything that you think is genuine, you should reflect that in the way you speak and in your actions as well. That's called being practical. There was a time such people were called *apta* in Sanskrit which is written like this आप्ता. Apta is he who thinks and speaks and acts in the same way. With time apta was changed to *aap*, the respectful form for 'you' in Hindi. For, "How are you?" in Hindi they say, "Aap kaise hai?" Ta has gone. Now there is another Sanskrit word called *shresht*. Shresht means a great person, a leader. That has become *seth* or proprietor today. No doubt we are undergoing change all the time, but we should not forget the aim and goal of life.

What is this problem with blood pressure? Who is putting pressure on you? What is this heart attack, who's attacking your heart? I laugh at you people. I have to drop my body as you will, but at least I am happy and you are not. How can you enjoy under the pressure of fear? All these couples here, you are not enjoying at all, even married life you don't enjoy. The best of the couples that you are, you are not enjoying. Why? Because you are under the pressure of fear of tomorrow, the future. How can you enjoy? Enjoyment comes when you are free from fear. And you will be free from fears only when you go beyond your mind. As long as you remain within the fields of your conscious and unconscious mind, you can never enjoy life; for the center of life, center of consciousness is beyond, that which is called individual soul.

Please remember, all of the body is in the mind, but all of the mind is not in the body. This is accepted fact. The Upanishads, the final and best part of the Vedas do talk about it, do discuss it, do explain this. Confucius, Buddhists, Zen, Zazen, they all explain it. Everyone found the same problem created by the mind. My mind does not create a problem for you. Your mind doesn't create a problem for me. Your mind creates a problem for yourself. That's why the Rig Veda, the most ancient scripture in the library of man, says, *tanureva tanno astu bhesajem*. O man, you have those qualities, and with the help of those qualities you can cure the diseases created by you.

What is medical science doing today? Every doctor is sick, and the sick are treating the sick and the whole world is a hospital. I'm telling you, this is true. I'm a medical doctor, I'm telling you this. The blind are leading the blind. Where will they go? They will go to perdition. All are experimenting, nothing is conclusive. That experiment which is accepted today, is discarded tomorrow. Nobody should say I am a scientist and my word is final. There is nothing like final so far. Therefore, we should continue making efforts to reduce suffering and make others comfortable. Somebody asked me why do all these hospitals exist? I said for the sake of hospitality! This is true. And even today we cannot extend our hospitality properly. One doctor goes to a patient with a great love and says, come on, cheer up, I will try my best to help you. And another doctor has no time, he gives pills and goes away. There will be a difference in the outcome between the two. Jar, one of the doctors, said that 50% of the diseases are cured by the way the doctor visits and treats the patient.

But I'm going one step further. I tell you that you are your own doctor. The day you understand it, then you will discover something great. There are healing potentials within you. You will come in touch with them when you have stopped becoming negative. Negativity is a very dangerous thing, and most of you are negative. If your husband is a little late coming home to you, stuck somewhere in traffic or in a bar drinking, or somewhere else, you get worried. What do you think? You don't think positively. You immediately think that he has met with an accident, or he has gone out with another woman. All these negative things you think, nothing positive. So your attitude towards life is totally negative and that's called self-created suffering. Why is a human being so negative, tell me? Why? There is 70% negativity in a human being, according to psycho-sociological data collected by Ameri-can society. They are wonderful in collecting data and very truthful.

You are all hankering for approval. You don't need society's approval. A wife always looks at her husband's moods. In the morning he says, "Honey you look nice." She responds, "You made my day." It's bad training from the very beginning. You don't need to lean on anybody for approval. That's bad. A day will come when he or she will go away. What will happen to that person who to-tally leaned on you their whole life? You are making that person miserable. Don't do that.

Suggestions, suggestions, everybody is blasted by sug-gestions. You are good, you are bad. Who are you to judge me? How do you know that I am good or bad? And you don't know yourself? Who is like this? A drunkard. A drunkard who is nude says to another nude person in front of him, "Hey, you're nude." He doesn't realize that he too is nude. In my opinion you should stop being nega-tive and start being positive. This way you will create a dynamic willpower which says, "I can do it, I am going to do it, and I shall do it." Instead, if you say, "I cannot do it, I am not able to do it," you are killing human potentials.

I'll tell you why cancer occurs. Suppose by chance your finger is cut and it starts bleeding. All the cells of your body start rushing toward the damaged part. In a few minutes' time you'll find that the bleeding has stopped. Why? Because all the cells rushed to that site of injury. But suppose those cells do not stop rushing, there will be a growth. That is called cancer. You can even prevent such diseases if you understand something that's called con-trol over your involuntary system. You know I sometimes think that I am so unfortunate that I feel like crying. All that I have done in my life, worked hard from the age of three, nobody wants to learn. People give me money, gifts, this food and that food, but nobody wants to learn. I think that if I have to be born again to teach you, it will be miserable for me, because I will have to work so hard all over again.

The human body has potential to cure its own ailments provided you know about your body. I don't discuss religion, so don't be afraid of me. No matter from which religious background you come from, I want to give you something which you need in your daily life. All the great bibles of the world say one and the same thing—be still, be still. For a few minutes in the morning and the evening, every human being should learn to be still. Why, because you will meet God? No, that's not necessary. You will be healthy. For your mental health it's important for you to understand quietness, stillness. During that time, those muscles which do not get rest even in sleep get rested. The voluntary system you can control. You can exercise and develop all of your gross muscles, but you don't have control over your involuntary system, the subtle set of muscles. For that you should learn to compose yourself, you should learn to be quiet, you should learn to be still, you should learn to breathe in a serene way. Scientists have realized that 70-80% of all diseases are psychosomatic diseases. They originate in the mind and are reflected in the body. These diseases are created by our bad thinking, negative thinking, passive thinking, not having control over our emotional life, not organizing our behavior, not understanding how to behave in the external world which is actually a very simple thing. Therefore, it's important for a human being, modern woman and man, to relax, to learn how to give rest to that part of the system which we normally do not know how to relax. Only 25% of the diseases come from the outside, are infectious or hereditary diseases. It means 75% of the diseases are not cured by so-called medicines.

So you are your own doctor. The school of meditation says that if you meditate for a few days, a few minutes every day, regularly, you will be not sick. This is called preventive cure. You have seen that there is research going on all over the world, research on cancer, stroke, heart disease, this disease and that disease. Prevention is better than cure. Now the endocrine gland system, chain of glands that secrete directly into the blood stream, is hardly known even by the experts. Very little is known about these glands. But who controls the endocrine gland system? Our mind. If the mind is put in a state of rest through meditation, even the endocrine system can be controlled. Our experiments in the Menninger Laboratory demonstrated that the mind can create cancer and mind is capable of dissolving cancer.

Now there is a word in the English language called gentleman. Actually, it has come from our Sanskrit word *manas*, which in Sanskrit means mind. Who are you? You are a man, gentleman. If you do not understand what manas, mind is, you do not understand anything about yourself. How can we have control over the mind? If you think that the mind is your enemy, either you make that enemy a friend or you can destroy that enemy. You don't have the power to destroy the mind. You had better establish friendship with your mind. You should learn to have a dialogue with yourself, a creative dialogue with yourself. Sant Tukkaram from Maharashtra did it, *manah sarvada bhakta ponthe bhi jayate*. "O mind, learn to follow the path of righteousness. Do not mislead me." As a friend, Tukkaram talked to the mind. You should learn to have a dialogue with your mind. This dialogue will lead you to understanding your mind. You fight the whole day with your mind. You know that battle, that inner battle, was the very cause and source of the Bhagavad Gita. The whole day you're fighting, from morning till evening. Either you give up, or you fight but never win. Have you heard of the Gita? Yes, Arjuna means what? *Arjun karne wala*, one who makes efforts, sincere efforts, is called Arjuna. And he who helps you is called Krishna. So there are two characters in the Gita and their dialogue is meant for all.

We have to find out the secret of polishing, taming, or learning to have perfect control over the mind which is the finest of all instruments. But only a small part of the mind can be grabbed. The totality of the mind doesn't come under our control because a vast part of the mind remains unknown to us. Many Easterners, those who have not studied Western psychology and philosophy, say, "Oh! Western philosophy is nothing, Western psychology is nothing." They are stupid. Freud says something very definite. Freud says that if the unknown part of mind is known, then you know all of the mind. Adler, James, all these psychologists tried to understand the mind. Whatever they understood, in a scientific way, is remarkable. What I learned from both, the interaction of East and West, is that the unconscious mind is like that iceberg which is hidden beneath the water, not known to us. The tip of the iceberg that is seen floating above the water is called the conscious mind, that which is hidden is called the unconscious mind. When we get closer we find that it is not actually the mind, it's a vast reservoir.

You say the mind is roaming, let it roam. Why are you bothered? It will never go anywhere. It will come back to you. Let it go, don't follow the mind. I once asked my Master, "How to practice?" He replied, "Mind tells you to go there, but you don't go. Tell mind, 'O mind, if you want to go, you're free to go. What can I do? But I am not going there.' " Fighting with the mind is never considered to be control. Therefore learn to lead the mind, make a certain route for the mind to travel and that is called learning to have control over the mind and it's modifications.

Now I'll tell you something about the kinds of problems that arise when you try to know the mind. A friend of mine once told me, "On this trail there is a ghost." It was at night but I did not believe him and I said, "I don't care. I've not seen it and I'm not curious to see it." We forgot all about this. After one or two months, I passed that way and it was a dark night. Suddenly I remembered that my friend had said that a ghost lived here. Even though I did not believe, why did I remember? Because anything that comes into my conscious mind finally filters down to the unconscious mind which is vast. The totality of mind should be understood, not only a small part of mind, the conscious mind, that we cultivate in our daily life.

Look here, mind roams around and you do not know what to do next. Many people close their eyes and they do not know what to do next. Mind will naturally run here and there. You always complain that mind runs away. No. If you know the system, mind will not run away. If you are trying to prevent the mind from thinking and say, "Mind, don't think," well, it's the *dharma*, the intrinsic nature, of mind to think. Mind means a catalogue of thinking, a series of thoughts. So when mind has a particular movement, you should simply learn to guide its movement according to your order. That is called control of mind. Not to think is impossible, but to think according to your plan is called an organized way of thinking.

Mind is a magician, don't listen to your mind. You should learn to educate your mind gently, and help yourself to one day have command over your mind. You should ask yourself, do you belong to your mind or does the mind belong to you? If mind belongs to you, you should learn to use it rightly. If mind belongs to your neighbor, let the neighbor look after it. If my mind constantly thinks of my neighbor and is jealous of my neighbor, it means my mind belongs to my neighbor and not to me.

People talk much about mind control, it has become a hot business these days. It's not enough to understand that I have mind and how to control it. Often people say, "I am going to teach you mind control." Nothing happens. In your life you should try to understand something about your body, your breath and about your mind; then it becomes easy for you to understand. I am presenting both views, the Western and Eastern. I have been living in the United States for almost twenty-five years and before that my whole life was spent in the Himalayas trying to understand life with its values, with currents and cross-currents. What I don't understand, I will tell you, I'm sorry, I don't understand this. You can talk for hours and hours, but when you are practical you try to understand your mind. You realize that your mind is a great magician. You have to be patient in dealing with your conscious mind. Now you have to determine that anything that comes into your mind will not disturb you and you will allow it to go away. This way you start introspection and then nothing will affect you. Inspecting within is called introspection. Police arrest the criminal, the judge punishes, but the witness remains unaffected. You witness all the activity going on, you are not affected. With this approach you can go to the higher realms within.

You say mind is powerful, mind is always powerful by its innate nature. But powerful in which way? Towards being creative or towards being destructive? That's

the point. So you will have to train that mind. Your mind
and my mind are weak in front of a robber's mind. When
he robs someone, he robs with his full force of will, of one-
pointed mind.

A thief, a robber, is a better meditator than a swami.
There was a heap of gold behind a thin curtain. A swami
and a robber were both asked to sit before it. The robber
was concentrating on the gold. Poor swami was not, because he didn't care for gold; he cared only for God. Why
do you want to have awareness, constant awareness? Because you have come to the conclusion that constant
awareness will lead you to freedom, that which Buddha
calls freedom from all miseries and bondages, a state which
is free from all bondages. That's why constant awareness
is needed.

Firm determination is called sankalpa shakti in Sanskrit. "Today I will not move, I will not fidget, because
that will bring strain and stress to my body." Keeping your
body relaxed, with your head, neck, and trunk in a straight
line, breathe in a serene way and learn to watch your thinking process. Do not identify yourself with the objects of
the world, because this way you are forgetting yourself.
When any thought comes, you decide, "I am not going to
identify with the thought patterns going on in my mind. I
will only witness my thoughts. No matter what happens
during these moments I will be not disturbed, no matter
what happens. Let my preoccupations come forward later.
I do not want to be disturbed." This way you will not
identify yourself with the thought patterns, forgetting your
true nature. You are in the habit of disturbing yourself. So
you remind yourself consciously, I will be not disturbed.
This way, you slowly build your sankalpa shakti, determination. Sankalpa shakti is something great. You don't need
an alarm clock, you do not need a watch, your mind will

remind you immediately. Gradually expand your sankalpa shakti. If I want to do something, I have a desire to do it, but I cannot do it, and am unable to find the means to do it, there will be no willpower at all. In ancient times, the rishis, the great seers, always used to remember, "I am this, and I am this, and I am this. I can do it, I will do it, and I have to do it, no matter what happens." That is called willpower. If you want to do something, just do it. Stop thinking about it. Stop doing something else. Just do it, no matter what happens, at all costs. That will create your dynamic will and that dynamic will enables you to create wonders in the world.

Mind cannot be infinite. It has limitations. In one of the Upanishads, the Ishopanishad, it is beautifully stated, *anejad ekam manaso javiyo.* "A" means no. Where there is no movement, yet runs faster than mind. It's a description for the atman. It means if atman is everywhere, where can you run? Mind, a great instrument and tool, can create hell and heaven for man, yet cannot run faster than the soul, for the soul is everywhere, mind has its limitations.

Chatushtaya antahakarana. Chatushtaya means four. The mind, *antahakarana* or inner instrument, is known by understanding four prominent limbs of the mind. As you have four limbs, two legs and two hands, so the inner instrument has four limbs: *manas, buddhi, chitta* and *ahamkara.*

Take the wheel of a bicycle. The wheel rotates because of its spokes. If there are no spokes, the wheel will not ro-tate. Further, the spokes rotate because there is something that does not rotate called the hub. If that hub starts moving, then the spokes would not move. This human life is like a wheel. So this wheel rotates on the basis of the spokes manas, buddhi, chitta and ahamkara. This

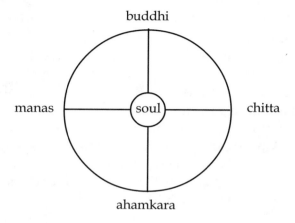

Figure 2

body moves because there are these four spokes within you. Now you want to know the nature of your soul? You can easily know with this drawing (*Figure 2*). In the center there is a hub. If that hub moves then nothing will move. That hub is called your soul, individual soul. What is the nature of your individual soul? It doesn't move, yet it creates all the movements. If this soul starts moving, all other movement will stop. Our individual soul is beyond all movement. All the movements are because of the mind. In the external world everything is subject to movement. Physics says, we are all moving, everything is moving. But there should be some center where nothing moves. Who is creating all the movements, yet does not move? That is the nature of the soul. Because of the soul everything moves, but soul itself is not subject to movement, because there is no power beyond the soul that can create movement in the soul. I'll tell you what the relationship between your individual soul and the universal soul is.

Your individual soul is like a drop of water, the universal soul is like the ocean. Qualitatively, they are one and the same. Quantitatively they are not. They need union and that's what we are all aspiring for. Why do we hate each other? It's because of ignorance. Why do you think that this religion is better than that religion? All the religions are one and the same, fundamentally. They differ only as far as nonessentials are concerned.

We have to understand these four functionings of the mind. Now, I'll give you a new analogy. A human being is like a busy factory. You businessmen will understand this analogy of a factory within you. In this factory, that which is responsible for importing and exporting is called manas. Shall I do it or not? Whenever you do something, that particular agent comes forward, shall I do it or not? I am getting so much commission, so much profit, shall I do this business or not? The nature of manas is always doubting, always arguing within yourself. That which decides what is good or not good for you is called buddhi. The entire set up is called chitta. Chitta is the storehouse of merits and demerits through which you receive all knowledge. All this power of thinking is coming from chitta. The whole factory is managed by ahamkara or ego. Then ahamkara, the I, says this belongs to me, this does not belong to me. See what is happening. Individual soul said, "Ok, Mr. Aham-kara, you become the manager." And ahamkara forgetting this, took over and said this factory is mine. That is the problem for all of you. Why are you miserable today? You are miserable because you have forgotten your proprietor and you think you are everything. That which separates you from the whole, that which separates you from the reality, that which separates you from the absolute is called ahamkara. The shortest cut is just to cut your ahamkara. When you learn to surrender your ahamkara, that surrender is the highest of all yogas. You can do it through prayer, through meditation, through contemplation. So far ahamkara is being used only for the external purposes. Surrender, used in a beneficial manner, when ahamkara is made aware of the reality of the soul, then that is called self-surrender.

I told you manas means that which has no capacity to decide. *Sankalpa vikalpatmakam manah,* one nature; another nature, *antarmukhi bahirmukhi,* it functions both within and without. Buddhi means that which discriminates, judges and decides; these are three main functions of your buddhi. You can term it in English as intellect. When manas consults the buddhi, buddhi gives a decision. Such a manas never commits mistake. So when you are performing some action, manas will always say, "Shall I do it or not?" Let the mind ask buddhi, that faculty which helps manas to decide. If you analyze your mind, it plays a lot of mischief. You go to commit a theft and manas, mind, will tell you, go on, go ahead. But manas will also tell you, if you commit a mistake, if you are caught, you will go to jail. Then manas will tell you, why not enjoy the privileges from the theft? Manas can only think, shall I do it or not, shall I do it or not? Then there is buddhi. If you commit a theft, you will be caught and go to jail, or, if buddhi is bad, if you commit this theft you will enjoy the results. Immediately the decision will be given by your buddhi. All your decisions and judgements depend on the buddhi. So what do the wise do? They consult their buddhi and with the help of buddhi control their mind, that which is always flickering.

So the moment you realize what is manas, buddhi, chitta and ahamkara, then you know something about your mind. A yogi knows how to establish coordination between the four different functions of antahakarana. Then there is no problem at all. But if buddhi thinks something different, and manas thinks something different, ahamkara goes off by itself, then there is no coordination at all. As you need coordination of your limbs in the external world to be a normal healthy person, so you need to establish coordination within yourself by understanding manas, buddhi, chitta and ahamkara. If you learn to establish coordination between the four aspects of antahakarana, there will always be tranquility within. And that tranquility will help you to do right actions, beneficial actions. When you make your mind, all aspects of your mind, directed and make them travel inwards, flow towards your internal states, fathoming all the subtle aspects of life, then you become aware of the source within you, the infinite library within you.

Let us examine the conscious mind. Even if you do not go beyond the conscious mind, even then it would be very beneficial for you. Just sitting still is beneficial for you. The next step is how to deal with the conscious part of mind. First of all you should understand something about the conscious part of mind. The conscious mind is that part of mind which you use in your daily life, during the waking state. When you are awake, you are using that part of mind called the conscious mind. That part of the mind which is educated by you, cultivated by you, by universities, by schools, it's but a small part of the totality of mind. Therefore, even though that part is trained, guided and cultured, the vast part of mind remains unknown to you. That part of mind which dreams, which sleeps, is not under your control. But even that part of mind which you are using now is not under your control. When you learn to understand this little part of mind called the conscious mind, you will realize that it is the gateway to the city of life and to that vast reservoir of the mind called the unconscious mind.

When I look at you, my optic nerve receives the image, sends it to my brain, then to my conscious mind and finally to my unconscious mind. And it is stored there. Now I may not see you for some time. When I see you again, I recognize you, because that form which I have stored in the unconscious reminds me that I have seen you before. So that reservoir within you, where you store the merits and demerits of your life, is very vast.

It's interesting to watch the part of mind which you are trying to train and educate and that part of mind which is helping you to do this. Slowly, you will find that your conscious mind is being expanded. And then you can allow all the thoughts to come up from the basement, from the unconscious mind, from the storehouse. But you should not get involved. Let us take an example. You are asked by your physician to go to the market to fetch some medicine for your ailing mother. On the way you stop at a red light. What do you do during that time? You wait for the green light. You do not go on counting the numbers of the cars, which make and what color. You just go on to get the medicine. On the way, you may meet your girlfriend, you may meet a very good friend of yours. What is your duty? Not to be swayed by these attractions, but to go to the drugstore and get the medicine. When you have a one-pointed mind, you may see someone you know very well, but you may not notice him and just keep walking to the drugstore. Because you are one-pointed in your mind and heart, there is only one thing that you have to do. In such a situation, you do not notice anything around you. Gradually, with this one-pointedness of mind, you catch hold of that part of mind which is not normally under your control.

Another point is how to cultivate the totality of the mind and become creative in the world, yet remain aloof and above. Is there any technique by which one can be free though living in the world? If you ask me I'll say yes. What is the way? If there is a way, it is only by going within, to the center of consciousness, from where consciousness flows on various degrees and grades. If I chew the whole Bible or Gita or any holy book, nothing happens to me. If I recite all the granthas or scriptures, there is no change. In my country, there are people who have learnt all the scriptures by heart. My father used to do the same thing. What is happening today is that practice is missing from our daily life. If we practice a little bit, we will experience. And that experience will become the guide and that guidance will lead us. May you all practice and at least have experience, a glimpse, so that such experience becomes your guide. If you are patient, you can easily learn to scientifically explore that part of the mind which is called the conscious mind. But you don't know how to control that part of the mind which is the dreaming mind or that which is the sleeping mind. Only a very small part of the mind is being used by you. But when you learn to expand the field of your conscious mind, finally everything comes into consciousness and there is nothing like unconscious mind. Learn to expand yourself.

Now, mind has two chambers: one is unconscious, another is conscious. Conscious means that which is used during the waking state. Are you awake? When you are awake then that part of the mind which you use is called conscious. That part of mind which you do not use, which is used during dreaming and sleeping, you do not know.

You see how pathetic a situation a human being is in. We boast about our learning, our wealth and our worldly wisdom. But we do not know. A very rich man suddenly dreamt that he had become a donkey. So the whole night he remained a donkey and was so miserable. In his dream, he told his wife, "I am sorry I got married to you. You are such a beautiful girl but I am a donkey." He totally forgot that he was a rich man, a husband, father, and respected member of a particular community. And his wife at the same time dreamt that she was a queen and her husband was a donkey. In her dream, she realized that it was a mistake to have married him. In the sleeping state, they slept and shared the same bed but they did not know each other. They were dead to each other. They were not aware of each other, of their children, the things they did and shared. They were not aware of any of that.

So you are using only a small part of the mind. You do not know how to use the dreaming part of mind or the sleeping part of mind. Great sages knew this technique, that's why they are called great. That which you consider great in the world, name, wealth and all this, yes it's necessary for you. But they renounced all that just to realize. They devoted all their time, their lives, to know and to have perfect control over that part of mind which was active in dreams and that which was active in sleep. The totality of their mind came under their conscious control. Before we did experiments at the Menninger Foundation in Kansas, no one could ever believe that the system which is called the involuntary system according to Western science, could be brought under voluntary control. But after the experiments, all the scientists began to believe that there is nothing like the involuntary system, that everything can be brought under conscious control. Many of you are confused about one thing. If you are a scientist or physicist, you will not talk about the mind but will talk about the brain. If you are a psychologist or philosopher, you will talk about the mind and not about the brain. But you have both. Brain is like a bulb, mind is like electricity, and the wires, the network of wires is like the nervous system. The nervous system is a channel for the flow of electricity. If the bulb is broken, there is no light even if there is electricity and the wires are intact. Or if the bulb is good, but if there is no supply, then too there is no light. So for proper functioning, there should be perfect coordination between all three.

Freud likens the unconscious mind to a bag. You do not know, you are carrying a bag all the time. It is like your shadow. Wherever you go, your shadow follows and will not leave you. You are always carrying that huge bag with you. Anything that you think goes into that bag. You do not know that part of the mind. You are trying to understand your mind, only a small part of the mind. You don't know the totality of your mind, both conscious and unconscious. If you know how to train the vast part of mind, the totality of the mind, you can do wonders on the earth. Anybody who has done wonders on this earth, anybody who was considered to be a great man, was great because he knew his mind. You do not have to know the soul because it's already there. In all conditions, the soul is there. What you have to know is your mind, and that's why you are called hu-man, your own mind. And the moment you know the mind, you can go beyond the mire of delusion created by your mind.

How do you approach that part of mind which is not known to you? First of all, you should try to work with the known part of mind. Suppose you catch hold of my finger. What will happen? My whole body will be motivated to protect this small part of it. And unless you release my finger, I'll do my best to release it from you. So too, you can approach the unknown part of mind by grabbing hold of that which is known.

The first point is to know how to be here and now. Second point is that when I dream, I don't have control over my dreams. Even if I want to dream according to my choice, sweet dreams, as you call them, I have no control. If you wish me sweet dreams, I'll say please don't wish me something bad. I don't want to waste my time in dreaming. You have no conscious control over your dreams, over that part of mind which dreams. You have no control over that part of mind which sleeps. The vast part of mind remains buried, remains unknown. Only a small part of mind is being cultivated by you and you are puffed up with pride that, "I have a Ph.D., a D.Litt., I have education, I have money, I have a car, I have all this." What is my point of view? Human beings are members of a fools' paradise. I go around the world and I see many, many intellectuals. But I find none of them practical and I cry. I don't say that you should accept whatever I tell you. I'm just making you aware that a vast part of the mind remains unknown to you. Now there is a third point. That which you consider peace, happiness, and bliss, where does it live? Where does it exist? If it was anywhere in the world, Americans would have found it first. They have even gone to the moon. Where is it? If mind is within, peace should be in the mind, or known by the mind, or known by understanding the mind. What is mind? Now let me tell you something. All of the body is in the mind, but all of the mind is not in the body. How will you know that part of mind which is not in the body? Therefore, to know mind is very important, not to know God because He is already there. You don't have to know Him. Body is already there, you don't have to know much about it. But you have to know the mind. So what the scriptures say, *mana eva manushyanam karanam bandha mokshayo*. By understanding the mind you can be free from all bondage.

With these simple ideas, you can be free from so-called stress. Even in the battlefield, I've asked my students to make experiments and let me know. Those who were dead were dead, but those who survived wrote to me. You can compose yourself even on the battlefield. What is the principle of karate and kung fu? Attention, just attention. You don't divert your mind elsewhere, just one-pointed mind. By making your mind one-pointed and inward, and going to the source of light and life which is the fountainhead of life within you, the center of consciousness, you experience a great joy. Then you can enjoy the world, you can enjoy all the things of the world. But if you don't have the capacity when you rush with all your desire to enjoy something, you soon get exhausted, you don't have the energy. You want to enjoy, but you don't have the energy, you don't have the capacity. You have desire, but no capacity. Therefore have a desire to enjoy and expand your capacity by learning the simple laws of holistic living.

It becomes easy for one to follow a path if that path has got milestones, so that you know how far you have come and how far you have to go. If from the very beginning you systematically study, follow this path, then it is not difficult. I think I should give you a small schedule. If you know how to sit and spend one month, ten minutes a day for a month, you will come to know many things about yourself. When you sit, the body starts moving. These movements are disturbances. After a few days you will not find gross muscle movements or body movements, but then subtle muscle twitching will create problems. When the body does not shake, does not move, is not twisted from this side or that, when muscles do not throb, small muscles do not twitch, then the body settles into stillness. That stillness gives you great joy. The joy of physical stillness is quite unusual, that joy is not found elsewhere. That joy is entirely different from anything you have experienced so far.

Can you attain that state of mind, that state of wisdom here and now? I say yes, you can do it. I have witnessed a few, not many, but definitely they have done it, and you can do it too. Don't leave your home in the morning unless you do some exercises and then some breathing, and then meditation. Ten or fifteen minutes is enough. Don't follow the Hindu way, Buddhist way or Christian way. Don't get involved in that. Tell yourself, "I am practicing meditation for getting freedom from stress. Because of my ignorance, because of bad food, bad relationships, I am creating stress for myself. I have to be free from stress. And for that I am making effort, for that I am practicing meditation." Soon you will find that you are experiencing joy, that you are free.

CHAPTER SIX

Emotions

Today, there is chaos all over the world, not because there are no intelligent people, no emotional human beings or no healthy persons. What is the problem with our human society? Despite many experiments conducted on three levels — mind, body, and matter — we have not been able to create an integrated human being. We have not understood the importance of an integral way of life. The power of thought and the power of emotion are both great powers. For total integration, we need to know how to use the power of emotion and how to prevent the mind from being disturbed by our emotions.

You may have heard this analogy. Once there was a lame man. He couldn't walk. He had no crutches, he had nothing at his disposal. And there was a blind man. Both wanted to go to the same village. They started talking to each other, "Is there a way? We both have the same destination." And after discussion they found a way. The lame man climbed onto the shoulders of the blind man and guided him to their common destination. So too should the power of thought and the power of emotion combine forces to achieve an integrated way of life.

It also means that after introspection and proper understanding of the various aspects of your internal states, you can all find solutions in life. Learn to think, not to brood or to worry. Have clarity of mind. Don't become a worrier, become a warrior. All problems can be solved because all these problems are self-created. As you are responsible for creating your problems, you have the power to be freed from these very same problems.

Now, virtually all our actions are controlled by our thoughts. And all our thoughts are controlled by our emotions. You may be a cultured and highly educated person in society, but suddenly a single emotion upsets you and you start doing things that should not be done. One emotion can disturb your whole being. You spend so much time and energy in culturing, in cultivating, in educating yourself. Yet, one single emotion can disturb you and make you a monster.

Therefore, let us find out why emotions disturb our entire being. Let me explain. There are six main emotional streams arising from the four primitive fountains of food, sleep, sex, and self-preservation. The first, the primary emotion is desire, also called *kama*. Kama is the prime desire from which arise all other desires. If this desire is fulfilled, you become proud and this is a serious problem. If it is not fulfilled, then you get angry (*krodha*). What is anger? Unfulfilled desire is called anger. The desire is not fulfilled, that's why you are angry. Your husband wanted you to do things in a certain way and you have not done it. He's angry. Or you are angry with him because he did not come home on time. Unfulfilled desire means anger. "Why are you angry honey?" he asks. You tell him, "I told you to bring something for the children and you forgot to bring it. You started drinking with your friends and you forgot. I told you not to drink and you are drunk, that's why I'm angry." Anger means unfulfilled desire. If kama, desire, is not fulfilled you get angry. If it is fulfilled, you become proud (*mada*). And then you get intoxicated (*moha*).

Pride is not self-respect, that is a false notion. I think, "This table is mine." Is it? No, it belongs to this organization. I am supposed to use it. I am not supposed to own it. So what happens? You don't know how to use the things of the world and you start owning them, that's a serious problem. You are not enjoying the house, beautiful house in which you live. But you possess it, "My house, my house, my house." And then becoming proud, you get intoxicated and then you get attached. When I go, I leave the table behind and nobody will disturb me. But when my work is done, if I say that I am going to carry the table home with me, the organization will say, "Stop! This is not yours. What is wrong with you?" All the things of the world belong to Providence. Please use them. Don't try to own them. That's a serious mistake that you are committing; something wrong with your thinking, something wrong with your behavior, something wrong with your understanding. So, there is a formula: all the things of the world can be used by you but please do not get attached, because they are not yours, they are given to you. If with this understanding, wife and husband sit down, talk and discuss, life will be beautiful. Your home will be a garden of Eden, but you modern people do not have the time to do so.

Let me tell you a story. There was a doctor, a very famous and extremely busy doctor. He had three children. At five a.m., he used to get up and go to the hospital, coming home late at midnight. His wife used to look after the children. One day the children woke up at night, saw him and asked, "Mommy, who is this rascal?" So is the case with all of you. You don't have time for children, you don't have time for your wives. What are you doing? Why are you doing all this? Tell me. Why this competition? Because my neighbor has ten million and I have only five million. To make it ten million you are working hard, ignoring your wife and children. Don't do that! There is something that is called peace. Learn not to be attached to the things of the world. Attachment is the mother of all miseries.

Then you get jealous (*matsarya*). I once visited a Greek church in Minneapolis in the United States. It was my first chance to visit a Greek Orthodox Church, not that I believe in churches, mosques, and temples. My temple is, "Thou art That." You are my temples, living temples. If I have not learned to see the Lord in you, I will be very unhappy. A mass was being performed. The priest did all kinds of rituals that I did not understand but I could accept because of the difference in cultures. In front of me there was a woman. Behind me there was another woman. These women were jealous of each other and were always competing with each other. The woman in front was muttering to herself, "What does she think of herself? She is wearing a diamond that is bigger than my diamond. She is wearing this fancy gown. Who does she think she is? Next Sunday, I'm going to wear a better gown." She was talking to herself and was frowning all this time. And she was looking backwards and I was caught in between. So I quietly asked her, "Ma'am, who is she?" She replied, "She is my next door neighbor, a nasty woman. How do you know her?" I said, "I don't know you and I don't know her." I told the doctor who took me to this church, "All these men and women are trying to show off in the church. It's like a club." Wherever you go, you carry your mind with you. Whether you go to a temple, to a yogi or to a swami, anywhere, your mind is always with you. At least you should learn to understand what is good for you and help yourself.

One of the sages beautifully said, *tulasi sant svamba taru phoolphale parahetu ichetete pahan hane vuchetate phala det.* A good man, a man of wisdom is like a tree, a mango laden tree. When there are mangoes on the tree, the tree bows down and the children throw rocks at it. What does the tree do? Nothing bad. It gives them fruit in return for the rocks. That is a sign of greatness. That we can attain in this world. It can be done. Human beings have done it in the past, we too can do it.

After kama, krodha and moha, comes *lobha* or greed. Greed turns you into an animal. You are a human being, but greed makes you lose all your human potentials. However, of all the emotions, the most dangerous is ego. You know what is this ego? There is body, breath, conscious mind, unconscious mind, and the center of consciousness. There are four different aspects of the inner instrument called antahakarana, the totality of mind, namely manas, buddhi, chitta and ahamkara. Ahamkara, or ego, is the greatest of all barriers in going to the source of light and life and wisdom, in attaining intuitive knowledge.

The final barrier is ego. Have you read in the history of Muslim kingdoms? The king, the father brings up his child with great care and love, but the boy thinks, "Let me put my father behind bars, let me arrest him. I can then become the king." Ego problem! When you are egotistical, you forget your own people whom you love and who love you. That creates a barrier between you and the reality. That creates a wall between you and the truth. So kama, krodha, moha, madha, lobha, and ahamkara, these are the six emotions arising from the four primitive fountains. If you understand a little bit of the anatomy of the inner person, the one within you, it will be easy for you to enjoy life.

I have seen you living, but I have not seen you enjoying life. Ok, is it necessary for you to have objects in order to enjoy? That means you are a slave of these objects. Nowadays, you talk of love, man needs a woman, woman needs a man. That's not necessary. You should learn about love without an object. So when you talk of something higher, about wisdom, it's love without an object and that sets you free. Freedom will come to you when you have organized yourself.

What is misery? Can you give me your misery? I am prepared to take it. No, you cannot because you have created these miseries for yourself. Will you please help yourself? It's a simple way. Don't try to become miserable. Buddha said, "Ye light thy own lamp, nobody will enlighten you." If people become miserable, it's because they want to be miserable, they want to create misery for themselves, there is no remedy. I will tell you how. Now do you exist? Everybody will say, "Yeah." I say you don't exist because I am blindfolded. I am speaking the truth. That's what we do to ourselves. There is nothing like misery, it is all joy, all joy. These are the various images of joy. Where is misery? Tell me what type of misery. What is its shape, what is its form? It is nothing.

Whenever negativity comes and you say, "I am bad." I say you are not bad. Who are you to condemn yourself? You belong to God. How can you be bad? Tell me. These negativities should not be entertained. You need to practice. Cleansing the mind, purifying the mind means not being negative, being positive, being realistic, being subtle, being practical.

You will have to work with your habit patterns. When a thief is caught, you ask him, "Do you know it's bad?" He replies, "Yes, I know that. I know it as you know it." "Then why are you committing thefts?" He says, "It's my habit." You'll have to learn to work with your habits. What are your habits? This personality of yours is composed of your habits. That becomes your character. But, if you start doing new actions consciously, repeatedly, you will create new habit patterns. You come out from old habit patterns and start new habit patterns. You will be transformed. It can be done.

Sankalpa shakti, determination, is the pillar of success. Don't condemn yourself if you fail. When a child starts walking, it falls many times. That does not mean that the child will not get up and walk. We have all fallen many times in our childhood but we are walking today. We are bound to fall when we start learning to walk. Determination is like that. If you fail in the beginning, it doesn't matter. Make efforts. Don't stop making efforts, that's very important. To know the truth, there should be truth in mind, action, and speech. And if you are committing mistakes in the quest of truth, you will be on the path, don't worry. Truth will support you, help you, if you are practicing truth. Don't worry about your mistakes.

These human prejudices hamper the progress of humanity. Only individuals, those who are aware, can do something in life and they can help others and we all have such potentials. Take some time, a few minutes in the morning and evening, and think about it. How can you improve yourself? How can you improve your personality? You cannot change it but you can improve it. Death has no power to change you, but you have the power to transform yourself. You have tremendous power.

CHAPTER SEVEN

Love and Relationships

There are two laws, the law of contraction and the law of expansion. Hate others, you are going through the law of contraction. Love all, you are going through the law of expansion. Learn to love, that is the law of expansion. What does love mean? It means to give, without any expectation, to your own people. This is a school where you learn to give unconditionally. Then you will learn that nothing is difficult for you, nothing is difficult. First thing you should learn is to just give. Instead of arguing with your wife, just give her what she wants. Just give your children what they want. Slowly, you will discover that they have started loving you so much and they have become so very considerate. They will never exploit your generosity. Learning to give is one of the greatest of arts. Give selflessly, to those at home, to those with whom you live. Start doing it there. Love will completely transform you, for love alone has that power, even death does not have the power to transform you. So if you love, then there is only love, there is no space for you. At present you have likes and dislikes; but with love, there is a sense of equality, you love all, you can never hate anyone. There is that underlying understanding that I will love all and exclude none. You are free. It is a joy that leads to bliss. There is so much expansion of your mind that anything that is hidden, that is unconscious, comes for-

ward as a part of the conscious mind. Why should you be
unhappy? You know who is unhappy? One who is selfish.
Who is happy? One who is selfless. It's that simple. I am
not telling you to go crazy, giving away all your wealth to
strangers, becoming uselessly charitable, no! I am telling
you to do experiments at home, with those who live with
you. Transforming your personality is the simple way to
attainment. Let us not make it difficult.

Your home is a miniature universe. Have you seen
the family of Shiva? You Hindus should understand this
symbolism. Shiva has got a deadly cobra around his neck.
His son Ganesha rides on a mouse. Is it possible for a snake
and a mouse to live together? Parvati has a tiger and Shiva
has a bull. A snake lives with a mouse and a bull lives with
a tiger. Man lives with a woman, a woman lives with a man.
It's a symbol of unity in diversity. O man, learn to adjust
your life in such a way that there is no conflict at all. You
can do that. Things impossible can be made possible, provided you learn to understand life. So Shiva's family tells
you that there are disagreements, disparities in life; yet our
goal is to be aware of, to establish the unity beneath all these
diversities. We can do this with prayer, by praying to the
Lord within you. Or you can do it with meditation.

There are always conflicts, confusion, with relationships in the world. A wife and husband, traditionally married and living together with all the amenities of life, claim
to love each other, yet remain frustrated. Why? Because they
do not understand themselves. How is it possible for them
to realize life and to understand the goal of life through
marriage? Girls and boys think that marriage is the solution to the problems of life. And they get very excited. The
girl thinks that one day the prince of my dreams will come
forward, I will get married and live happily ever after. The
boy also thinks that the day I find my ideal partner, I'll be

very happy. But, nothing happens, because a basic philosophy, basic understanding, basic knowledge, is missing. This is especially so with those from Eastern traditions. They bank more on the sayings of their books and
they talk about their ancestors. "Our scriptures are great,
our rishis, our sages, were great, our forefathers were
great." But how about you, sir? We have to understand
this.

We used to live in the mountains of India, the
Himalayas, that you have all heard of and many of you
have visited. One day, a prince from a nearby state, who
was educated in Oxford, came to visit my Master with all
his guards and secretaries. That morning I was standing
outside the cave monastery where I was brought up. The
prince came forward and said, "Come here, O *brahmachari*
(apprentice). Come here." I said, "What's the matter? Who
are you?" He said, "I want to see your Master." I said, "You
cannot see him. Don't order me around and get out of this
place." So his secretary came forward and said, "Do you
know he is a prince?" I said, "I don't care. I am the prince of
the Himalayas." The secretary now became very humble,
as did the prince, "Sir, can I please see your Master?" I said,
"Ok." My Master was sitting inside. The prince, affecting
the mannerisms of polite society, said, "Good morning to
you, sir. You seem to be lonesome." My Master replied,
"Yes, because you have come."

Don't forget who makes you lonesome, remember this
point. Those who claim to love you make you lonesome. A
foreigner, a stranger, does not make you lonesome. Who
makes you lonesome? Those who are closest to you. Because you expect too much from others, and others do not
have the capacity. Many young boys and girls think that
marriage is the solution for life. It is not. It is like a fortress,
those who are in it cannot come out and those who are out-

side want to get in, all with great suspense. One is a helpless state, another is state of suspension. In my opinion, we should all learn to understand something in our childhood and start training and teaching our children so that they understand something about life, learning to examine one's own self, then learning to relate with others. We remain strangers to ourselves and yet we try to communicate in the external world with others and that is not helpful. It is creating sickness. I have been doing experiments, I have been analyzing things, I've been watching, observing things very subtly. What do we do in the name of love? In the name of love we use others, we lean on others, we, instead of helping, hurt others, we injure others, we become dependent. Dependency is a sort of disease.

When you get married, have four understandings with your partner. We will not fight in the mornings, we will not fight before going to bed, we will not fight while eating food, but the rest of the time if we want to fight, we can fight. It's very injurious if you do not have such an understanding in life, such a simple agreement. If two people fight, I can stop their fight just like this. You know what I tell the wives? I don't call them housewives, that's a bad word. No woman is married to a house, so no one should be called a housewife. I tell them, please, when you are angry, the other person should understand that you are angry, and he should not lose his patience during that time. He should just remain quiet. Simple advice. When do you get angry? Not when you are balanced. You get angry when you are emotional, irrational. But what happens? Suppose you are angry, and then your wife also gets angry, and the children start crying, and even the neighbors also get involved, what will happen? This thought pollution that you are creating will go on expanding, spreading to the whole universe. So learn to understand that the individual family is something great, meant to radiate love to the neighbors, to the whole universe. And for that you need understanding. When your partner is upset, it is best to keep quiet. After sometime your partner says, "I'm sorry." But if you go on fighting that is not therapeutic, that's not healthy. I'm not saying that you should both sit in silence and not do anything. I'm saying two wheels of a chariot will lead the chariot in the same direction. And that is very good. Please fight but not all the time.

Don't fight with a woman, for you will never win. You will be sorry if you fight with her. Once, Nancy Reagan, the wife of President Reagan began to cry after a fight they had. President Reagan, the President of the United States, who had the power to press a button that could destroy the whole world, begged his wife, "Please Nancy, please don't cry. I, with all my powers, am at your disposal." But Nancy wouldn't stop. He used all his powers but he failed. Finally he started crying and Nancy said, "Don't cry, my boy. Now, you know who the boss is."

Learn to understand everything about yourself. It doesn't take much time. You don't need a swami, a yogi, a scripture or anything. Just be thoughtful. Sit down for few minutes. I have seen a husband saying sorry to his wife 100 times, because she was very calm. Whenever he got angry she remained calm. So after a few minutes he would say, "Honey, I'm sorry." But if a husband says sorry 100 times a day, he's a rat. He's no real husband. I find this type of imbalance everywhere. But if both are calm, understand each other and have this understanding, "Well honey, when you are upset, I will not say anything and when I am upset, please don't say anything. Let us have this clear contract." Then there will be no problem. But you don't want to sort out your problems. The great institution called the institution of marriage has become an institution of misery. I know, because I am a counselor. I have counseled 45,000 couples, and none of them were happy. And those who are happy, I adore them. Two wheels of the same chariot can go travel the road very pleasantly. It's difficult for a single wheel to do this. So in the world, two people can do wonders, provided they adjust, provided they understand each other.

Attachment is misery, nonattachment means love. First understand that. I am attached to this chair. Is it good? Because it is not mine, I don't have a right to be attached. I can use it. Husband is yours, love him instead of being attached to him, because a day will come when you two will be separated. It's nature. It will happen with everybody. Therefore, follow the path of love which is called non-attachment. Attachment brings misery, nonattachment means love that gives freedom. A little bit of understanding is needed. Mothers, you are the builders. You are the first architects of this world. This architecture has come from your minds. Don't forget that you are superior to men. You carry a child for eight to nine months. The power that you have, man does not have. If you put a small pebble on his tummy and tell him to walk for two-three days, he cannot do it. You are definitely superior. But don't be proud, don't get carried away with women's liberation. Don't forget that you are a great mother. When a woman became pregnant, she wanted shelter. She told her husband, "I need a shelter for my child. So far we have been irresponsible. I will have a tender child, how can I look after my child? I need some shade, I need a home." And he started building a home and gradually that thought became a school called the school of architecture.

Mothers, you are the real architects. This is your responsibility. Man is tired and worn out. You should wake up, get up and build our society. That which man cannot do, you should learn to do, because you can do it. A child's education is totally in your hands. The seeds which are sown in childhood are the real foundation for education. You have a great responsibility. You are definitely superior and higher than man. Don't have this complex that I am inferior because I am a woman. You have great powers. When we learn to understand this, we will realize that a great part, a vital part of our society is being misused. Women are being misused, exploited for marketing, for publicity, with posters and all kinds of vulgarity. We should be aware of the wealth we have.

In childhood, the mind remains tender. A tender bamboo can be bent easily but not a mature one. A child's mind is very receptive. All the seeds sown in childhood grow very nicely. You and I, if we now appear in a high school examination, will both fail. Childhood is something great. A child needs guidance. Actually, there is chaos all over the world in our educational systems. If we impart good education to our children, become selfless examples for them and give them love, perhaps they will grow, become the best citizens of the world and the whole universe will bloom like a flower. Education is very important. An old man is exactly like a child, but full of follies. Childhood is pure without any follies. So when a child grows, he grows with the education that has been imparted by his environment, education imparted at home which you call culture, education imparted by the college and the university. Parents should make some sacrifices for their child and work with the child. But what do parents do? Instead of giving education to the child, they give them their problems. "Do this, do that. If you don't do it, I'll spank you." The child is confused. The child grows but grows with many conflicts. I don't think we should impart such conflicts to our children, create conflicts in their minds. We should not do that.

The parents should learn to meditate and children will always imitate their parents. From childhood they will form such habits which will create their personality and that's what they become. So, from the age of three, children should learn how to sit in meditation.

An individual creates a whirlpool for himself. An individual is helpless. He has to perform his duties and when he performs his duties he has to reap the fruits. We all have to perform our duties, that is our intrinsic nature. I am not hindering the running of the world and the perfomance of actions. I'm just saying that we, as members of our society, should become responsible. We should learn to give away the fruits of our actions and continue to do our duties with this understanding. Anything that you assume in your life is your duty. You are born in a particular family, in a particular society, in a particular country. You have to do your duties according to your family, according to your society, according to your country and finally to all of humanity. This is what the Gita teaches. Then, society will bloom, the flower of society will bloom in a better way. There are two worlds, the world created by Providence like the sun, moon, stars, earth, and water, and the world created by us, by human beings. I am talking about the world created by human beings and not the world created by Providence. Let us manage the world created by us, let us not worry about the world created by Providence.

In this cosmic cycle of evolution, a time comes when you become a human being. Time is rotating constantly. There are other kingdoms that we have gone through, perhaps; no one knows, I don't know. When you have become a human being, you have a power, you are responsible for your own actions. What you do as a human being depends upon you. A human being has got three aspects: the animal aspect in the human being, the man in the human being, and the divine in the human being. All three combined is called a human being. The question is what degree of divinity is in you, what degree of the animal aspect, and what degree of humanness? You will have to analyze that. I am not searching for God. Really I am not because my God is in front of me — all of you. These beautiful faces belong to my God. Anything that dwells in you is my God. I am not searching for God. I am searching for someone, but I have not met him as yet. I am searching for a perfect human being. And wherever I go, I look for him, but I don't find him. So I am sad. I have visited 156 countries in the world. I have not yet met that man for whom I am searching. Let's all make the effort to become good human beings, to be good citizens, to love all and exclude none. That is the way to the divine.

I have seen something amazing. When I go to see many swamis, they always ask me, "Do you go into the world and see people, how are they?" They think about you, and you people think about them. So remain wherever you are, enlightenment has nothing to do with renunciation or action. You should learn to build your concept of life and it's not very difficult, it is your birthright. No matter what cultural background you have, which religion you belong to, if you have not built your personal philosophy, it's not going to help you. Every now and then, great men come and give a push to humanity as a whole, to help them attain the next step of civilization. What do they do? Can you create a flower, a leaf, a blade of grass? No. The flowers are the same, but these great men change the basket, according to their times.

A good yogi who has received a glimpse of this knowledge starts working with himself. Not by running away from the world, not by abandoning his duties, not by renouncing but living in the world yet remaining above. You know what is your symbol? Your symbol is beautiful, it's called a lotus. A lotus grows in the water and mud, yet remains above. I don't have that symbol. I am a swami, that is not my symbol. You are definitely superior to me. A householder's duty is not at all inferior, provided you remember the symbolism of the lotus.

CHAPTER EIGHT

Prayer and Contemplation

There are four approaches to attaining the purpose of life: the school of prayer, the school of contemplation, the school of meditation, and that of selfless action. I will systematically explain these schools so that you understand the differences between them and, according to your own choice and capacity, you can follow one of the schools and finally attain the goal of life. Let us first try to understand prayer and contemplation.

I've seen that prayer can solve that which cannot be solved in any other way. Prayer means closeness to the Almighty, to the absolute truth, to the source of energy, to the source of strength. When you pray whole-heartedly, your mind and heart run one-pointedly to the source. During that time you become an instrument of that power, you become a channel of that power. If your prayer is genuine, it helps. If your prayer is egocentric, it does not help. These are the two sides of prayer. If your prayer is genuine, if you are very selfless, anything that comes out of your mouth helps. If you are not genuine, if you are not selfless, your prayer, no matter how many times you bless others, is useless.

Prayer is always answered provided it is done correctly. There are two types of prayer, egocentric prayer and God-centred prayer. Egocentric prayer, is called *sakama prarthana, sakama upasana, sakama bhakti,* that is desire-filled prayer, desire-filled practices and desire-filled devotion. Egocentric prayer makes you very poor and petty and you cannot go beyond that. "O Lord, give me this. O Lord, give me that." All the time you are begging. It makes you a beggar, it never improves your life because you're feeding your ego all the time. It is not considered to be a great prayer. Sometimes it is answered and sometimes it is not, because it is just to feed your ego. Otherwise all prayers are answered, answers which you do not receive from any other quarter, from anyone else, because life itself is a big question mark. No matter how much one explains, yet there is a question. Every individual has a question and that individual wants that question to be answered by someone higher, greater, one you call God. You pray to God, but that prayer should be God-centered prayer. Do not ask anything from God because God already knows your needs. There is difference between need, want, wish, and desire. Our days are laden with wants and nights with desires. Thus we remain disturbed all the time and put the blame on God and say, "I suffer thus, because of the Lord. It's He who makes me suffer."

Just as karma is a law, prayer is also a law. Prayer can help you by strengthening your determination, so that you do not perform those karmas which create barriers for you. When you start establishing proprietorship of the worldly things that you own, that you think are yours, you create problems for yourself. You then pray, "God help me." How God can help you, I don't understand. This prayer is of no use because we are constantly creating a whirlpool for ourselves and then praying to God, "God liberate us." This kind of prayer is called egocentric prayer. Such prayer does not help.

The school of prayer is unique and wonderful but it

should be God-centered prayer. The right prayer is not a prayer that goes, "Father, give me this, give me that. Father, I want a good car. Father, I want a good wife. I want this, I want that." Prayer that makes you aware of the reality within you is the right type of prayer. To become aware of the reality, go to the deeper aspects of your being, to the source from where you get energy, from where you get strength.

How to conduct God-centered prayer? Lead me from the unreal to the real. Lead me from darkness to light. Lead me from mortality to immortality. *Asatoma sada gamaya, tamasoma jyotir gamaya, mrtyorma amritam gamaya.* Three desires are expressed in the prayer. Lead me from untruth to the truth. Untruth, means this apparent reality which seems to be real but is not. It's not absolute, not real. Lead me from this to the ultimate truth. Lead me from darkness to light. Dispel all the ignorance that is created by our karma, our mind, our action, our speech. Lead me from mortality to immortality. So far we are aware of the mortal aspect of life. A human being dies and then you do not know anything about what happens after that. He is born, he grows, becomes a youth, grows old and then he dies. There is another aspect of life and that is called immortality. Lead me from mortality to immortality, my Lord. So there are three prayers. The first prayer is to be led from apparent reality or untruth to absolute reality, absolute truth. Second, darkness to light. Here darkness is symbolic. Darkness means ignorance. We suffer on account of ignorance. Buddha said *avidya*, ignorance, is the mother of all problems. Let us be free from this ignorance. Who created this ignorance? It's not created by God. It's created by our own actions, by our own thinking, by our own understanding. The third prayer is for total spiritual wisdom, leading from mortality to immortality. Lord, lift me from this physical awareness, this worldly awareness, to the highest awareness that is called spiritual awareness.

Prayer is not conducted in Sanskrit or Arabic or English or Latin or any other language. Prayer should be conducted in your own language. Which is your language? It's the same language in which a newborn baby speaks to her mother. It's the language of love. You see how a newborn baby communicates with the mother. Speak in any language, the child will have nothing to do with it. But when the mother says na, na, na, na, na, chu, chu, chu, chu, chu, she communicates well with the child. Which is that language? The language of love. When our mind, our thoughts, our emotions, our whole being is integrated, when our mind and emotions go together, when we become one-pointed and with that feeling we pray, that prayer never goes in vain!

Prayer gives you strength. The highest of strength is received from that source which is already within you, through prayer. When you pray, whom are you going to pray to? The God Almighty who is everywhere? No. The Lord who is within you, seated deep down, beyond your body, breath and mind, in the innermost chamber of your being. Your prayers are always answered, when you pray in your own language, with mind and emotion joined together, with a one-pointed mind. You can pray at any time, but you should learn to discipline yourself. Morning and evening hours are considered best for prayer. But as I told you, pray directly to the Lord of life who's seated within you. Gently close your eyes and with all your feelings and thoughts ask the Lord of life to give you wisdom and there you will find strength.

There are two balls; the ball of clay is flattened when it falls but the ball of plastic bounces up again. Those who pray have strength. Those who do not pray, have little strength, they are weak people. You see people who live for a cause are fearless because they have a cause, they have a goal in front of them. They don't know what fear is. They have an aim in life and they pray to the Lord. They believe in the Lord who witnesses all our actions, speech, and thinking.

You should always learn to forgive yourself. Prayer and repentance purify the way of the soul. Self-realization leads you to your goal. Sit down and if you think that you have done something bad, which you shouldn't have done, don't repeat it and you are free. Don't condemn yourself. "I am bad, I am bad, I am bad." This self-suggestion will strengthen guilt which is not healthy for you. The sense of guilt is strengthened when you go on repeating the same mistake and then accept your helplessness, that you cannot help yourself. "So what if I committed a mistake? I am not going to commit that same mistake again." Then at that moment you are free. No matter what happens, don't accept defeat. Don't do what is not to be done and you are free.

Do not condemn yourself and say, "I am so bad, I am so dirty. I don't have the capacity to pray." This type of self-condemnation leads to sickness and you lose self-confidence. Learn to forgive yourself when you commit mistakes. Now the scriptures prescribe a beautiful way to be free from the stains of the impressions within us called *prayashchitta*. It's very simple. Prayashchitta means repentance, means a determination not to repeat your mistakes. Then you are free. But instead, you go on repeating those mistakes and then go to a church or to a temple pleading, "Lord forgive me." And then, you again commit the same mistake and again plead, "Lord forgive me." You may commit the same mistake many times. You need strength, inner strength. O man! you need strength. O human being, you need strength! And that strength is not external strength but strength from within. Prayer gives you that strength. Then you can easily go through this procession of life smiling, not harming, hurting or injuring anyone. You can march, jump with joy all the time. The school of prayer is valid.

What is faith? You bought an apple orchard with the expectation that you will get fruits. You paid for the land and paid for the fruits. But after you had paid for the land and fruits, did you pay for the shade you are enjoying there? You take the apple in your hand and start eating, sitting under the shade of the trees. No you have not paid for the shade. When you talk of faith, faith in what? I have a body, I have this faith. What do you mean by faith? Faith does wonders, reasoned faith does wonders, that faith which is not challenged by the mind is a great faith, faith in which mind and heart should become one. Heart is the center of emotion, mind is the center of thinking. When mind and heart, emotion and reason, are put together, trained together, then that faith is unchallenged, nobody can challenge it. But faith without reason is very dangerous, it's blind, it's not a safe crutch. It may help but it does not lead.

I told you prayer is very good but egocentric prayer is not healthy. God-centered prayer is definitely healthy. It makes you aware of the reality within yourself. I once met a minister of the church. She was a woman, a very famous woman in the United States. She invited me for tea. By chance the remote control for her garage did not work, so the garage door would not open. She said, "Jesus, please help me open the garage." Jesus did not open the garage. I said, "Is Jesus your servant who will open the garage door?" She said, "I am going to open the garage. I'll show you a miracle." I said, "Perhaps you have another remote control." She said, "You don't know my powers." I said, "I want to see." She could not open the garage. "Jesus, you are angry with me." I said, "Why is poor Jesus being dragged into such a mundane thing?"

What do we do? We pray, "O Lord, give me a car. Hey Lord, give me a good girlfriend so that I can get married. O Lord, give me a good husband." O Lord! Everything you want is mundane. And He says, "Ok, I'll give you this candy, I give you this candy, I give you this candy." And you are bribed with these candies and you cannot go beyond. If a child cries, the mother says come on take this candy. But if the child throws the candy away, finally what does the mother do? She'll pick up the child. There is no other way. Therefore, there is something great in *tyaga*, sacrifice. "I don't like this, I don't want this, I am not satisfied with this. I want the best, I want you mother, I don't want anything else." With this determination, we can attain the goal of life here and now.

Why is *japa* done? Just to see that there is no space between thoughts. Your mind has three conditionings: time, space, and causation. Now see the space between these fingers. If there is no space between them, there is only one. If there is no space, there will be no time, there will be no causation. If you are constantly aware of the truth, there is no space between your thoughts. Many thoughts will come and go, but beneath there is only one consciousness. That is the easiest way to use the mind. Otherwise, the mind is such a small scale with which you are trying to measure the whole universe, it's not possible. Now you can go beyond.

There is something beyond that which you consider sanity. You call it insanity, but there is definitely something in insanity. I was at the University of Allahabad, writing a book, doing research on a particular book which is considered to be the most difficult and terse book of Vedanta. You cannot pronounce its name, even after hearing it three times. It's called *Khandanakhandakhadyam*. Very difficult name. I found out that the Vice Chancellor, Mr. Jha, considered to be a great, learned man of the country, had not written a single original line. He drew one line from here, one sentence from there, one paragraph from somewhere else and made a book. I was very sad. I went to him. I said, "Sir, may I ask you a question?" He said, "Yes?" He was sitting in a revolving chair, big chair. I said, "Why are you cheating people?" He said, "What's the matter?" I said, "You have taken one paragraph from here, another paragraph from there, and you have become learned. This is theft. There is no originality in it." Do you know what he said? He said, "Son, originality is only found in an asylum." So I kept quiet.

Once, I wanted to know how people live in an asylum. I went to visit the asylum in Agra. The previous day, Mr. Nehru, the Prime Minister of India at that time, had also visited the same asylum. I found the people of the asylum in a world of their own, amazing. So I started talking to them. One said, "Who are you?" I said, "Just a swami." He said, "Swami or slave?" And I wondered how sometimes wisdom comes from such people. I said, "I heard that Nehru came here yesterday." He said, "Oh, anyone who comes over here calls himself Nehru." I said, "No, no, he really was Nehru." He replied, "Who cares who comes and who goes, we are here. That's all." I asked them, "Do you believe in God?" Some said yes, some said no. You know what one of them said? He beckoned to me and said, "Hey, here, wait. Whether you believe in me or not, I'm still here." But one of them said something very remarkable. He was a lawyer and he was not at all crazy. His brothers had him committed because they were afraid of him, that he might create problems with division of property as they were very rich people. He said, "Do you do japa?" I said, "Yes." He said, "That's not needed." I said, "Why?" He said, "God is your father, right?" I said, "Yes." "Ok," he said, "suppose you keep calling out to your father, 'father, father, father, father, father, father, father, father, father, father,' from morning till evening, what will your father think of you? He'll be annoyed, fed up with you. He'll think you are crazy. Do you think God is happy with your japa? Doing japa is of no use," he said. That gave me food for thought. "If you don't listen to what your father says, and you don't act according to his instructions, but keep saying all the time, 'father, father, father, father, father, father,' as you keep doing japa all the time, are you not crazy, swami?" I said, "I have to think about it. Thank you, thank you for your teachings."

Why do you do japa? Why are you repeating the same thing again and again? With japa, that mind which normally wanders into the external world with the help of the agents called the senses, becomes one-pointed and then inward. But if one remains limited to only japa, then really, one remains crazy. To expand your consciousness you have to learn to meditate and it's an art. It's not part of any religion. If you want to know yourself, which religion is it? It's called religion of man. You have to know yourself, you are introducing yourself to yourself. Normally, you behave in a false manner, a fake manner. Husband says, "I love you honey." Honey responds, "I love you too." All fake things. Because if someone asks, "Who are you?" You reply, "I don't know." Therefore, to understand oneself on all levels is very healthy and that's our birthright. Understanding ourselves on all levels is called meditation. That's the point. And there is a system for it.

There is another school called contemplation, *shravana manana nidhidhyasana*. What is contemplation? Contemplation is to discover what truth is. I am in search of truth. I listen to the sayings of great sages and to the scriptures taught by competent teachers. This is shravana. I think deeply about these sayings and teachings. This is manana. I systematically go on searching and finally, I know truth and integrate it into my life. This is nidhidhyasana. And I cannot describe it to anyone.

Be nice, be kind, be gentle, be loving. What is new about what you are studying, tell me? Have you read anything new anywhere? You have learned ten words for one word, is that improvement in your knowledge? Then what is that knowledge which we are trying to explore and understand today? My whole life, my mother, my father, grandfather, my teachers, everyone says, "Speak the truth," and I do not know how to. That's a very serious problem. I would like to speak the truth, everyone wants to speak the truth but nobody teaches you how. You see at home, children are spanked by their parents when the children lie. But after ten minutes, the child finds that Mommy is lying to Daddy, and Daddy is lying to Mommy. The child is confused, "Is it a rule for me not to lie?" So the child tells her brother, "We are not allowed to lie. They are grownup, they can lie." We don't find good examples in our childhood. All aspects of education are given by the institutions of the world, except one education called exemplary education, where you learn through example. We suffer on account of this lack of exemplary education.

Now, what is happening in your families? No matter how many lies you speak from morning till evening, you spank your children, saying, "Always speak the truth." No matter how great a liar you are, you don't want your children to lie. The father constantly lies, mother constantly lies, and child is confused. He thinks that my parents have a license to lie, but I'm just a kid, I don't have that license. This is true. So he's confused. How to practice truth? No mother or father ever teaches the children that. You don't teach them how to speak the truth. This is the point because you do not know yourself. So, for ages there is this myth, "Speak the truth, speak the truth, speak the truth." This is all nonsense, it's a principle, it's not practice. It happened with me. I was confused in my childhood. My Master never spanked me, but others spanked me and everybody said, "Hey, speak the truth." I said, "Look, I am not what you think, don't touch me." But I was a kid. I said, "Tell me what is that truth." Nobody ever told me that.

One day I was very upset and I told my Master, "You have ruined my life." He looked at me and said, "I brought you up, I educated you, I gave you so much love. I don't want to hear such a thing from you. Do you ever find me selfish?" I said, "It's not a question of being selfish or not being selfish. My life has been ruined by you." He said, "Why? What have I done to you?" I said, "I am still ignorant and a fool." He said, "I tried my best to teach you, but you have not been able to learn." I said, "What you are teaching me today,'Do this, do that, do this, do that,' that's the same thing that all mothers at home teach their children."

I told my Master, "I know that I should speak the truth but I don't know how to. Will you please teach me? Show me how to speak the truth." He taught me that the simple way of speaking the truth is by not lying. If you do not lie, you are speaking the truth. But if you are trying to speak the truth and you do not know what truth is, then you are making your own truth. You say my truth is my truth and I am speaking the truth and you should listen to me. That is confusion. Do not lie. By not lying, you practice speaking the truth. Do not do what is not to be done according to your conscience. By not doing what is not to be done, you start doing what is right.

Practice is different from the principle. It's easy to say, "Don't do this, don't do that." Learn to practice. Don't give up your practice. If you are defeated by others, it doesn't matter; but if you are defeated by yourself, that's a very bad thing. Then you are helpless. No one can cure you. There are diseases which cannot be cured by anyone when you become helpless. "No medicine is helping me, nothing is happening to me, I am going to die. The world is so gloomy." When you become totally negative, you cripple your willpower. Don't allow that to happen.

In the school of contemplation you learn what is truth. Now you want to contemplate on that teaching. Truth in the world is different from absolute truth. If I go to a shop, what does the shopkeeper say? "I speak the truth, that this costs $12." You buy it. Actually it doesn't cost $12, it costs only $6. He's selling it in the name of truth and you are buying it in the name of truth.

Avidya or *mithya* means falsehood, yes, untruth. Untruth, in which context? Untruth in the social context or untruth in the absolute context? There is nothing like untruth as far as absolute truth is concerned because absolute truth is everywhere. *Idam sarvam khalvidham Brahma.* This is all, everywhere there is truth so there is no place for untruth. Once Mother Theresa was asked, "Do you believe in evil?" She answered, "I do not have time to think about evil. So, sorry I cannot answer your question. How can I believe in evil when I think of the Lord all the time with mind, action, and speech?" There is no mithya as far as absolute truth is concerned.

The teacher explains that scriptures say that you should learn to speak the truth, you should learn to do truthful deeds, you should learn to be truthful in your mind. Is it a new teaching? We are so swayed by our culture and each others' suggestions that we have completely lost our individuality. We hardly get time to think, to understand, and to act according to our thinking. Even if you want to speak the truth, you cannot. Others will not allow you to speak the truth. Yes, it happened with me. When I started doing experiments in the United States everybody was very happy, all the scientists, even the religionists. One day they found out what we have done. They thought, "He's injuring our religion. His work is getting so much importance. That's very bad." Then they started attacking me. They wanted to undo what I had done, but it was scientific work. We are so full of prejudices. After the second world war, Americans did not want to do research with Germans whom they had defeated.

Therefore, the great wisdom that is deeply buried in the great scriptures teach *vidhi* and *nishedha*, what to do and what not to do. By not doing something you start doing that. My Master taught me, "Don't go around telling people to speak the truth and don't claim that you speak the truth, don't say that. Simply, don't lie." By not lying you are speaking the truth. Now I found that you cannot lie. Please tell me one lie and I will tell you that you cannot lie. You say, "Swami Rama is a donkey." This is not a lie. Donkey is something, Swami Rama is something else. You are simply a fool in saying that Swami Rama is a donkey. A human being possibly cannot lie, he's merely not relating with the facts. From the very beginning teach your children to relate with the facts, to be very practical and not lie. Don't try to prove that this chair is a table. With argument you can. Don't do that. Learn to relate with the subject. This way our society can become a poem, a song. I'm not talking about one individual. I am talking about the whole society.

Truth has a great power. It can be practiced by not lying. What is a lie? What does it do? It creates a great, serious division in your heart and mind. You know that this is not a cot, it's a chair; but you are trying to prove that this is a cot. Your speech is different from your mind. You are hurting yourself, not others.

So yoga science says you are constantly blasting and hurting your inner being by lying. Don't do that. By speaking a lie you don't hurt others, you hurt yourself. When you are afraid, you lie. Don't tell others, "I am a good person." You don't have to say that. Let your conscience be the witness. When you start practicing, you'll find that to speak the truth and do truthful actions will make you strong and healthy, will make you a great man. One can stand as an example, a head of the family, who can be an example. If children know that Daddy lies all the time, they say "Daddy, I love you but you are a liar. Mommy, you lie the whole day but I get a spanking when I lie. That's not fair!" And after some time, children will not respect parents.

Satyam bhruyat priyam bhruyat na bhruyat satyam apriyam. A blind man is coming by. We both know that he is blind. I cannot say, "Hey, you blind man come over here." That is *apriya.* It is truth, but that truth is vulgar because you are hurting somebody. So the *yamas* or restraints of yoga science are *ahimsa, satya, asteya, brahmacharya* and *aparigraha.* First yama is ahimsa, comes before satya, or truth. Ahimsa, '*a*' means no, '*himsa*' means harming, hurting, killing, or injuring. First, we should have that understanding that no matter what we speak, what we do, what we think, the basic foundation in our relationship is that we should not hurt, we should not harm, we should not injure, we should not kill. And only then we talk of truth. So, these are expressions of love. Nowhere in the world, no scripture ever explains the way of expressing love. Only yoga manual says that ahimsa is an expression of love. If we are followers of the same path we can get along with this understanding. And if we are not followers of the same path, there is no need for such a compromise. Do not compromise with falsehood. Otherwise you'll be wasting your whole life.

Don't hurt, don't harm, don't kill and don't injure. By not doing this you are expressing your love. This is called a negative virtue. By practicing this you are loving. At home, please don't kill, harm, or injure those whom you love. Start from there. That truth which hurts is not truth. Therefore, don't say that. Suppose somebody is running this way and the police are chasing him. You have no business to say he is going this way. Why do you want to get involved? "O police, I am telling the truth, the man went that way." Suppose that man is innocent? This way you should train yourself. Truth means relating with the things of the world. Absolute truth is absolute truth. But truth in the world is entirely different. So don't hurt others.

A few hints for practice. Don't speak too much. Those who speak too much speak nonsense most of the time. Speak less, to the point. Reduce, if you are speaking too much. Be conscious that I will not speak much. Second point, "Ok, I will speak whatever I have to speak but I'll speak strongly and lovingly." Don't keep saying "I mean to say, I mean to say, I mean to say." Many people say, "I mean to say." It means there is something they mean to say, that they are not saying. Be straight, be gentle when you speak. Your speech will be effective. Those to whom you are speaking will know the language, it will affect their hearts and minds if you speak properly. We have done many experiments. These days it's a problem to communicate with human beings. It's easier to communicate with animals. This was the problem in ancient times also. Rishis say, *ahimsa pratishthayam tatsannidho vairatyaga,* Yoga Sutra. These great seers, rishis, did not believe in violence, they knew only how to love. Even animals abandoned their cruelty, their violence, in front of such people. This is true. Strength lies in love not in violence. Violence is a weakness. May you learn to be strong because strength means love. Do not be weak. That is not love.

Slowly by understanding the great sayings of the sages, you start contemplating the great sayings, "I am atman, Brahman. The atman is within me. I'm not body, not the breath, not the mind, not my individuality but the atman within me is the same *Paramatman.*" This type of contemplation, constant awareness, is very healthy.

CHAPTER NINE

Meditation
and Selfless Action

On the temple of Delphi it is written, "Know thyself." How can you know the self? There are two diverse approaches. Western philosophy says go from the gross to the grosser and then to the grossest aspect of life. That is the Western approach. The Eastern approach is to go from the gross to the subtle and then to the subtlest aspect of life. Both are searching for unity in diversity. There is no difference. However, it is easier to go within. Because if you go within, there is no chance of getting lost. If you go outside, you may get lost. You may become a victim of worldly charms and temptations. Therefore, the simple way is to learn to sit still and go within. You don't have to call it meditation, you can give it any other name.

Man has made many experiments on mind, matter and energy. These experiments have been made because man wants to attain another level of consciousness, a higher civilization. He is not attaining it because there is so much disparity. Those who have attained look like fools in the world and those who have not attained look like they have attained. If we really want to attain the next step of civilization, a higher civilization, then we should learn to look within, find within, and be within. This exploration is missing. I do not say that there is nothing outside, no, no, no.

So far, do you think that the knowledge you have received in the external world, is called right knowledge? This knowledge, received through your sense perception, and by your conceptualization and analysis is limited. This knowledge is important only for dealing with the external world, the world of objects. There is another library within you called the infinite library from where you receive knowledge. That knowledge does not need verification. You will never need to ask your husband, friend, boss or anybody, "Am I right, sir?" Because you know it and know that you know it. And there is no conflict, and you don't need any evidence. That state of mind seems to be the very state of contentment, it brings and gives you great contentment. Therefore you should learn to meditate.

All the schools in the world and your parents teach you how to behave in the external world, how to have education from this school and that school and how to become a professional, a scientist, a philosopher or a businessman. Real schooling comes when you become aware of yourself, when you start questioning life, though living in the world. I have all the amenities of life, what next? Am I happy? What next? Then you become a seeker of happiness, a seeker of truth, a seeker of bliss. So, you say Lord help me and He helps you.

When truth is universal, Brahman is universal, how is it possible for you to be excluded from that highest truth which is everywhere? It means, He is in you and you are in Him. Then where are you? Your existence is not your existence. So the moment you come to know this truth you are free from all bondages, from all ignorance, stress and strain. Therefore, O man, realize that the kingdom of God is within you, the Lord of life is the highest of all. Anyone who has realized this, would like to go to his innermost self. And there is a way for that. I am not talking about Hinduism, I am not talking about Buddhism, I am not talking about Christianity, I am not talking about Islam. I am talking about something universal. The moment you realize that the absolute truth which is not subject to change, death, and decay is within you, then you attain a freedom, freedom from fears, all fears. That is called the state of enlightenment and that can be considered to be a state of perfection. Therefore, learn to go to the deeper aspect of your being. Everyone should learn to meditate so that he's free from many, many diseases. That meditation should be simple, a purely scientific technique, without putting any brand, like Hindu meditation, Buddhist meditation, Zazen, Zen meditation, Christian meditation or Jewish meditation. These teachers have destroyed the whole philosophy of meditation. Meditation is a simple method.

If your meditational technique is not complete, let me assure you, you cannot go far. What happens? There is a serious weakness among the teachers and gurus these days. They will put a color on it, my meditation, that teacher's meditation. Meditation is meditation, they put a brand on it. Thus they disturb the system. This is a system that should lead you beyond your body, senses, breath, conscious mind, unconscious mind and then to the center of consciousness which is called soul within you, the main source of light and life within you. You do not need any religion to support your meditation.

Who taught meditation for the first time? Indian woman. I am going to give you that history. Outside every village there is a plaza with a well. Indian women go there in the evening to fetch water, balancing vessels of water on their heads. Women like to speak to each other about their pains and express themselves. They will dance, cry, laugh, discuss family problems with each other, but their vessels will not fall off their heads. This is called meditation in action. You do your duties no matter where you go, whatever you do, but you do not forget your atman, the Lord seated deep down within you. So no matter what you do, the consciousness should not fall. Who is the founder of the school of meditation? Not man, but woman, remember that.

Long ago in China, there were two vehicles of Buddhism that traveled from India. One through Tibet, and another through Southeast Asia. That vehicle which traveled from the north is called Mahayana, the great vehicle and that which went through the southeast is called Hinayana, compact vehicle. Nobody in China knew anything about meditation. So this Buddhist teacher sat against the wall for fourteen years meditating. That attracted everyone's attention. What is this? How it is possible for a man to face the wall and meditate thus for fourteen years? They asked, "Which religion do you come from?" He said, "Meditation." Everybody was surprised. That school of meditation became very famous. Meditation is actually not a part of any religion. It is exploring yourself, exploring the deeper aspects of your being, and finally leading you to the center of consciousness within. Anywhere you bifurcate, you mingle any other thing, then it's not meditation, you are disturbed. There is no chance for you to come in touch with the negative part of life if you are doing meditation correctly.

Many of the western religions are afraid of the word meditation. Meditation means a journey without movement. In all journeys of the world you have to move and then you go forward. But there is one journey where you do not move, yet you go forward. That is called journey without movement. You first learn how to sit. The Bible says, "Be still and know that I am God." Something great!

What a simple saying, but how difficult to apply. How will you know God? The easiest way to know God is to look within, to find within, to be within. But the Christians and Jewish people don't follow this. How to be still, that's the point. How to be still? What is that stillness? If I tie you with a rope to the trunk of a tree to make you still, will you become still? What it means is that without being still, you cannot know the truth, that's the point. First of all you should learn how to be still.

But no Christian follows it, nobody wants to be still. No church teaches you how to be still. I've been around the world, visiting many churches, they don't know how to be still. "Swami, do you know how to be still?" I said, "Yes, that's what I learned in the Himalayas." "But you are a Hindu," they said. I replied, "A swami's a swami, he's not Hindu or Christian or Muslim, he does not belong to any religion, he's beyond all religions." "Oh! Then I want to learn." I love Christianity, but what disturbs me is churchianity. I love Islam, but what disturbs me is fanaticism. I love Hindus, with their great scriptures, immense wealth, but they never study them, they never follow them. These orthodox religions are enveloped with the dust of ages, and they are not helpful to us, they don't touch the corners of our daily life. Therefore we have to learn to understand life with all its currents and crosscurrents.

When I went to Salt Lake City, I was invited to a monastery because I was a monk and they were monks. And we had very frank discussions. Wherever I am invited, I share my joy and partake of their joys. When my turn came, I said, "All of you have studied the Bible, right?" They said, "Yes." "Do you practice?" They said, "Yes, literally, we practice." I said, "Jesus says, when somebody slaps you, turn the other cheek. How many of you have done it?" None of them had. I said, "Can you tell me the meaning of this? I give you twenty-four hours to think about it. I am here as your guest." They said, "But you are not a Christian." I said, "How do you know? How do you know that I'm not a Christian? Perhaps I'm a better Christian. So after twenty-four hours we will decide who is a true Christian and who is not." So next evening, we renunciates re-assembled and they said, "We cannot tell you." I said, "It's a very simple question. Who is that man in life, whom you can slap and he will give you the other cheek? A child sits on the father's lap and slaps him and father gives him the other cheek and the child goes on slapping. Nobody does it except a father or mother. It's a simple answer." They said, "Yes, you are right." When you have become a father, then you can tolerate the kicks and blows of the world, nothing happens to you. That's the meaning of this. Practicality is missing from religions, that's why nobody is following religions, no one.

The school of meditation is systematic and therefore suits people like scientists. The method of meditation should also be systematic. If it is not systematic, if it is abrupt, if it is colored by some religious myths then it could be a negative sort of meditation, then you come in touch with your negativity. This means your method of meditation is not systematic. Systematically follow the inward journey, a journey without movement. In this journey you have to be still and quiet. That is called meditation, learning to sit still. You have to prepare yourself to learn not to move. From your childhood onwards you are taught to move. Nobody teaches you how to be still. Yoga science teaches you, gives you some practicum, says, learn to be still by being steady and comfortable. For a few minutes every day you should learn to practice this, everyone should. It's very therapeutic.

A few minutes of meditation, then prayer and then contemplation. Fifteen to twenty minutes of meditation will help you, will help you throughout the day. But if you meditate one day and say it's enough for a week, that's not good because there is no food in the world that lasts you for a whole week. Confucius beautifully said that if you do not meditate regularly, if you miss a day, you miss a year's progress. Learn to meditate every day. All the joys that you have experienced so far are nothing compared to the joy that you derive through meditation, the greatest of all joys. You go to the source and from there you come out with that joy. So learn to meditate.

Patanjali, the codifier of yoga science, a great master of meditation, instructs his students, *satu deergha kale nairantarya satkara sevito dhrudda bhumi.* "O student, learn to sit every day at the same time." Why? Because it will be easy for you to form a habit. Today your mind travels in certain grooves and every day the mind is traveling through these grooves. And you do not know what to do with your mind. It's an old habit and you do not know how to change this habit. Many times you know that it is not good, yet you do it. You drink, you know it's not good but you cannot break that habit. Why? Because your mind leads you into the grooves of your habits. What do you have to do? You have to create new grooves for the mind to travel in, instead of those old grooves. Mind stops traveling here and starts traveling there. Repeated actions create grooves in your mind. Repeated new actions will create new grooves. So meditation is conscious effort. It should make your mind one-pointed and inward. It's very pleasant. That which leads you to your negativity is called suggestion, it's called hypnosis, not meditation. That's the difference. I will tell you the difference between these two. You are suggesting, "Go to sleep, go to sleep, go to sleep."

This is called auto-suggestion. Your doctor says, "Now you are sleeping, you are sleeping, you are sleeping." That's called hypnosis. Hypnosis has two sides, somebody hypnotizes you or you hypnotize yourself.

Prepare yourself, in the morning after a wash, sit down for a few minutes. Let the people at home know that Daddy meditates or Mommy meditates. It influences children. Do you know that if you record the thought waves of a sleeping child when you meditate you'll find they are different? Even your pets are influenced by your meditation. It even affects your plants at home. It's a very powerful thing. It sends out good vibrations to all. If you are a meditator and think that you are going to be harsh to your husband after meditation, you cannot. You go to your *puja* room and pray, and then say, let me give a bit of my mind to my husband, you will not be able to. It's very good for the wife and husband relationship. It's very good for father and son's relationship. There is a great gap between a growing son and parents these days. And the mistake lies with the parents, not the sons, because they want to control their son and the son wants to grow independently. There is a generation gap. But when you learn to meditate, you will perhaps understand. You will understand yourself and you'll understand others. You don't understand others because you don't understand yourself. Please start meditating.

You talk of silence. Have you ever realized what silence is? Have you not seen a mother at home asking her children, even her husband, "Please be quiet. I want you to be quiet for some time. I'm tired of doing my duties. Will you please leave me alone for some time?" Every human being wants to be alone for some time. That being alone does not create loneliness for you. Loneliness is very dangerous. It's ignorance. But that being alone means being all in one. That you like to be. Why do you not regulate your day and decide that you will not leave your home unless you meditate for a few minutes every day? There are some important exercises called exercises without movement. You can do them at home, in fact in your bedroom. Even if you are very lazy, you can do those exercises. Be aware of your diet, then do some breathing exercises and then start doing some meditation. The last part of meditation is called real prayer. Meditation is compact prayer.

Now, what is this meditation, meditation on whom? It's a very simple technique. First learn to sit straight in the easy posture on the floor, keeping your head, neck, and trunk straight. If you cannot sit on the floor, you can sit on a chair with your hands on your knees. Gently close your eyes and systematically survey your body from head to toe. Your mind will tell you which part of the body has some strain. You'll find there is some physical tension which is related to your mind, your emotions. So you are surveying, relaxing every part of the body systematically, going down to the toes and then coming up to the crown of your head. Attend to your breath after that. Push in your abdomen as you exhale, which helps your diaphragm to expel the carbon dioxide, the used up gas. When you exhale, feel as though you are exhaling all your problems, worries, and pains. When you inhale, inhale as though you are receiving energy from the atmosphere. And then do not think of breath and mind, go beyond, and watch your thinking process. A thought comes and goes away. Let it go. Learn to inspect, this is introspection. Be vigilant. This way you will find that thoughts which are coming from the basement of your mind, the unconscious part of your mind, where you have stored many impressions from your daily life are not affecting you. You are being a witness. During that time your mind, nervous system, fine set of muscles, all the tissues and cells will get perfect rest. Of course meditation is a technique that leads you beyond this witnessing of your thoughts. Even if you cannot go beyond, it's very healthy to sit still. Any method of meditation is helpful, healthy and very, very useful. Learn to sit quietly and teach your children to do so also.

Learning to meditate means learning to explore the dimensions which are not known to you. Many aspects of your personality are not known to you. You are wonderful. Anything that is considered to be bad is not yours. It has come from outside. Anything that is good is already yours. Examine this, this is true. The school of meditation is healthy, therapeutic and calming.

The highest of all joys on this earth is meditation. After all worldly joys what happens to you? You are tired. What do you do? You go to bed, you say you want to relax. What type of joy is it that makes you tired? All your joys finally make you tired and then you want to sleep. When a fool goes to sleep does he come out a sage? No, he comes out a fool. But if a fool goes into meditation, he comes out a sage, he doesn't come out a fool. So there is difference between sleep and meditation. Sleep is an unconscious act, you get rested, a part of you is rested, but a part never gets rest. That's why you look tired, you feel loss of energy.

So consciously if you learn to go beyond that state which is called sleepless sleep, that is called meditation, it's wonderful. You don't have to run away from home, you don't have to go to a monastery, go to a swami or to a guru. Just learn to sit down wherever you are at home, regulate your life for a few minutes in the morning and evening. Make it a part of your schedule, it's very helpful. Even if you just imitate the process, it will help you. Suppose you are not doing meditation, but you are sitting quietly. The autonomic nervous system and the finest muscles will get rested. When a mother is sitting in meditation, her child comes and sits, imitating the mother. Do you think the child is meditating? No, but I say the child is meditating better than the mother. Even imitating meditation is very helpful. Make efforts, conscious efforts to have control over your mind. It is very healthy, very therapeutic. It will bring you in touch with that dimension of life which is not normally known by you. Don't leave your home unless you meditate for few minutes every day. The moment you wake up, sit down in meditation.

Meditation is very easy provided you learn meditation from someone who himself has been trained on the path. Meditation has two purposes. There is a human reservoir which is termed kundalini according to the scriptures, and there is a technique that is called sushumna application. If you have learnt many breathing exercises but if you have not learned sushumna application, it's not helpful. Sushumna means *sukha mana*, joyous mind. To apply sushumna means to create a condition for the mind so that mind is joyous and wants to go inside instead of going outside. Mind has formed the habit of going outside, to the outside world, to the world of objects. Mind does not want to go inside to the world without objects. Here you make the mind inward, you follow the journey without movement. It's a great joy when you learn to do it correctly. And you don't have to sit the whole day and become a swami or yogi. Early in the morning, as well as in the evening, when you have completed your duties and the sun starts going to bed, at the wedding of day and night, sandhya, you can sit for few minutes and learn to understand, to compose yourself, to go into that silence where you receive everything.

You have to know how to make your body still. A few days you will find that the body rebels. When I first went to the West, they asked me to come and speak at Los Angeles, at the university. Everybody was shaking like this. I said, "What are you doing?" Their teacher said, "Our kundalini is awake." I said, "If I don't speak the truth, it's not good. But if I speak the truth it's bad too. What to do?" I said, "Look here, if you are moving like this, in a drugged state, and then say kundalini is awakened, forget it. This is not kundalini." That latent power, energy in you, when it awakens, it goes through various centers and it's scientific. I understand that, but there is a system for it. You don't drug yourself, then start hallucinating and call it kundalini awakening, no! Some of them agreed with me, some of them left because they were drug pushers. Don't go towards hallucination.

If there is no disturbance, then you are in meditation. If there is disturbance, if you are hallucinating, expecting, desiring, then that's not meditation. Signs and symptoms of meditation are calmness, happiness, and bliss. Suppose you fight with your wife. But if you meditate, even imitate meditation, after that you will not like to fight with her. It's a concrete symptom. Those husbands who are great fighters, they should learn to meditate. Those wives who are great naggers, they should learn to meditate. It's very healthy for you.

We try to hide our insecurities by wearing good clothes, by being vain outside, though full of fears inside. It's true, we all have that split personality, dual personality. No one knows us because we don't want them to know a part of ourselves. The real part of ourselves is never known to us. We are three selves, the real self, not known; a part that we don't want others to know, our petty, so-called weaknesses; and the face or mask we wear for others. For example, how free you are in the bathroom. You have no clothes on, but you are not ashamed because you are by yourself. Then you wear a loose gown in front of the family members. But to go out, for a wedding, you wear very fancy clothes. But if your husband were to say, "Honey, please dress the way you dressed up for the wedding always," will you be free? No. All the impositions of wearing this and that are not to your liking. You are playing a role for others but you are not happy playing these roles in the external world. You feel that you are missing something. In reality you need to understand yourself on all dimensions, and for that you should learn to go within yourself, because that no one teaches you.

You say that I have been doing meditation for a long time, nothing has happened. That's not possible. That's untrue because it's against the law of karma, it's against science. You throw a rock somewhere, will it not hit something? How is it possible for that rock to vanish in thin air? Not possible! When you are doing something, you're bound to reap the fruits. If you are truly meditating, you will certainly be benefited. But what do you do? You sit down and then get annoyed with your wife. "She has not cooked the meal properly on time, she doesn't listen to me." And the wife is going, "My husband doesn't care for me." What you do in the name of meditation is not meditation, my dear. You are afraid of your wife and so you cannot say any strong words to her. So in meditation you are doing all this. I once put a hidden camera and I told twenty students to sit and start practicing. In one minute's time, their facial expressions changed fifty times. Their thoughts were affecting their facial expressions. When you sit down for meditation, determine that I will not allow myself to be disturbed by anything. That is why there is prayer. Prayer gives you that strength. "O Lord of life and the universe, please help me, give me strength." Pray for a few seconds and then start meditating. Keeping your head, neck and trunk straight, take some deep breaths and start meditating. It's a method of going inward, journey from gross to subtle, and then to the subtlest aspects of your being. If you make sincere efforts, you'll find that the disturbances that you had to face in the beginning like body movements, are slowly disappearing. Body is now still, breath is serene and slowly mind is becoming calm. If you do something half-heartedly, if you do your business half-heartedly, can you expect good results? No. So is the case with meditation.

How is your individual soul related to the cosmic soul? If you understand the philosophy of life, it will become easy for you to practice and understand the role of individual life in our society and then understand the purpose of life here and now. You want to realize God or the Self of all. A human being is great because God dwells in him, lives in him; the highest of all truths, absolute truth, dwells in him. And wherever he moves, that truth, God, has to move with him. But for lack of self-realization, he suffers. All suffering comes from lack of self-realization.

There was a father, a widower, who was lonely and used to drink. He took to drink because he kept remembering his dead wife. He missed her. So he went to the bar and did not return home till two a.m. and the son got worried. The son went to see what had happened to his father. The father was sitting all alone, drinking. The son said, "Father now let's go home, it's two in the morning." He said, "Son, when those two people leave, I will also go." The son said, "But father, there is only one."

So when you are intoxicated, you see two instead of one. I see so many faces because I am intoxicated. Beneath all these beautiful faces, there is only one unity. To be aware of that unity, freedom from that intoxication, that's meditation. When I start meditating, I will not see many faces. Beneath all these beautiful faces, I will see only one unity, one life force. Meditation will lead you to unity, not to diversity. This diversity is because of hypnosis. This is the difference between meditation and hypnosis.

I rarely speak in churches or temples, excuse me, I don't. Because for me, you are all temples. According to my philosophy every human being is a temple. Which temple is higher than you? If I do not see God in you, and then go to the temple and search for God there, I am not loyal to the Lord, I am not faithful to my Lord. So I directly speak to the living temples that you are. I always make you aware that you are the greatest of all living temples. All these conflicts going on in the world, religious conflicts, will vanish the day human beings understand the real philosophy of life that every human being is a living temple. We should learn not to harm, not to injure, not to hurt anyone and that will be the day of enlightenment for all of us.

I am not against your going to a temple. I think temples, churches and mosques, are community centers, they are essential for communities, but I don't think they will benefit you much religiously, because you ignore yourself and then go to the temple. What is a temple going to give you? You are a living temple yourself. Please don't misunderstand me, I also believe in God, but I do not believe in God the way you do. If you want to see the President of America, and say, "I am a beggar. Will you please allow me to come into the White House and meet President Bush?" You will be not allowed to go near the President. You have to be a president yourself if you want to see the President. You have to realize yourself before you meet the Self of all. This is truth and there is a systematic understanding, study and technique. You do not need to retire from the world and go to a Himalayan retreat for realizing the Self. Thou art the greatest of all wonders. The greatest miracle is that infinity dwells in you. You are a finite vessel and you are carrying infinity within. It's the greatest of all wonders. You are speaking, you are listening, you are thinking, who is giving you that power? That's why I always say, O man, you are greater than God because God does not have man in him, but you have God in you.

With this understanding you should learn to be very, very practical with yourself. Just try for two-three days, not more than that. I will not speak that which is not to be spoken. I will not do that which is not to be done, according to my own ability. I will not entertain those thoughts which are injurious. One of the great French writers said something beautifully, "If a good thought is not brought into practice it's either treachery or abortion." How is abortion treacherous? Ask a woman. For one who understands something about life, if he cannot translate his good thoughts into action, it's something very treacherous.

What is the goal of life? The goal of life is not to be God, and not to see God. It's all God. God never created this world. The most ancient scriptures in the library of man today are called Vedas. The Vedas say, *prajapatischarati garbhe antaryayamano bahudhavidhayate.* The Lord of the universe did not create the universe, no. Then how did it come into existence? The One became many. It manifested, was not created. Where is God? This is all God. Why are you searching? For which God are you searching? This is all God because this is all a manifestation of God. Who else can manifest except one absolute called highest reality or absolute reality? Now, with the help of mathematics which is considered to be the very basis of all sciences today, you can come to the same conclusion. Pick a number, say 92. This 92 will not exist if there is no 1 in it. It will become 91. There is only one absolute and if you repeatedly use that one 91 times, it becomes 91 and then 92. There is only one absolute, which has given all these beautiful faces. Nay, these are the faces of only one absolute. But a human being, because of the dissipation of his mind and its modifications does not assimilate this truth. He roams around in the external world in search of peace. He experiments but he doesn't obtain that peace.

Now let me give you a picture of society. What is happening with us? Either our mind goes to the grooves of the past, or fantasizes about the future. You will never find yourself if you do not know what the 'now,' the present, is. You are misusing human potentials because you are not trained, nobody trains you and you are not training yourself. When wife and husband fight, husband says, "Honey, be happy, I'm taking you to Singapore day after tomorrow." She's so happy about going to Singapore. Then some family problems come up and they forget about day after tomorrow. Day after tomorrow never comes. Poor honey, she was very happy for only five minutes. What do you do in your daily life? You postpone your happiness. Yes, this is true, because you do not know how to be in the present.

What is missing in your life? The now is missing. You do not know what 'now' is. You know the word, you know the meaning, but you do not know what it is. Because your mind knows only how to travel in the grooves of past experiences and how to go forward into the future. Is there any method that helps you to be here and now? It's important. If you go to the church and pray, "Lord, put me into the here and now," He is not going to do that. If you go to your neighbor, he is not going to help you. Who's going to help you? You will have to learn what that 'now' means. 'Now' is part of eternity. What will happen the moment you come to know 'now'? If anyone knows this 'now,' he knows past, present, and future. And he's free. And anyone who does not know 'now,' cannot know anything, no matter how much astrology he knows, no matter how much he talks.

You don't have to search for the teacher. When a student is ready, the teacher appears. If you are not ready, teacher will not come even if teacher is there. *Kabira beech bazarme charliyo laptay dekhana hara chalegaye pankhiliyo uttay.* A diamond was lying enveloped in dust on the roadside. Nobody cared. They thought that it was a piece of glass that was glittering and shimmering. But a jeweler came along. He knew right away and picked it up saying, "It's not glass. This glow is from a diamond." When you are prepared, the teacher will come. Don't worry about the teacher. Don't search for the teacher. Teacher has to come, this is Providence. Make your best efforts. Don't just pray, "Now will you please show me the light? Will I have light?" Even if the whole universe prays for you, you will not have light. You will have to open your eyes to see the light.

Every human being needs therapy. In today's world, I have not seen anybody who is not suffering on account of stress, except one person, Swami Rama. I have no time for it. You have enough time to think useless things, so you suffer. I don't have the time, I enjoy. I don't want to come back. Technique alone is not going to help you. You have to build a concept.

When your body becomes calm, there will be turmoil inside. You should know what to do next. So in all the systems, you climb step by step. It's like a ladder with many steps. One by one you climb the rungs and finally reach the roof. You and I see the horizon through a small window and conclude that the horizon is so small. But a great man comes, says no, no, no. Come here, I'll take you to the roof where you'll see that the horizon is vast. It depends upon your perspective, from where you are seeing. Gradually start working with yourself, you will go to the next step and then the next, and so on. I am happy that you are doing it.

There is something beyond this also. I light a lamp. Please pay attention to this. For some time, I protect the lamp from the gentle breeze. But when that light starts growing, it grows to a forest conflagration helped by the same breeze. When you are weak, you need support. But when you have become strong, adversity also helps you. There is nothing like negativity then. In the beginning you need that moral support, you need that inner support. That's why you go to this person and that person and consult the scriptures. Scriptures and lectures inspire, but practice alone leads you to that.

If this room is dark for 100 years how much time will it take to light it? One second. Let us not go towards that defeatist philosophy. If I am looking at the sun and walking backwards, I will never see anything. I will have to go in the right direction too. As long as we believe in theory and not practice, then we'll suffer. I have had many experiences in my life where I can say that there is an invisible power that helps me. And why only me? Everybody. If we don't drink, perhaps we'll not meet with an accident. So accident is our karma, our foolish actions lead us to this chaotic condition. If we learn how to do our actions skillfully, lovingly and selflessly, we'll never suffer.

That's why it is said, *svese karmanya garbha samsidhim labhate naraha.* We all should learn to discharge our duties and by discharging our duties we will go towards perfection.

As a human being, do you lead a liberated life or a life of bondage? If you study the lives of great men, there is one characteristic that you will find in their lives. They were all selfless, everyone of them. Those who practice, practice this point first. I'll be totally selfless. Once you become selfless you are free from attachments. There is freedom on many levels. There are two worlds in which you live today. There is the world projected by nature, Providence, the world of sun, moon, stars, earth, stones and rocks. Then there is the world created by you: this is my home, that's not my home, this is my wife, that's not my wife, these are my children, those are not my children. The world which you have created and superimposed over the world created by nature, binds you, not the world created by nature. First you will have to seek freedom from that world which you have created for yourself.

Freedom, freedom, freedom. What is that freedom? One freedom is freedom from the bondage of karma. Second freedom is freedom from mental confusion. Final freedom is to make a clear concept in life and thus be free. So there are three steps, three levels of freedom. First we'll describe what is that bondage of karma. You have to study a law which is called universal law no matter which community you come from. This is called the law of karma. Whether you are a Hindu, a Christian or a Buddhist you'll have to follow it. As you sow, so shall you reap. *Avaseva bhoktavyam krutam karma subha subham.* You'll have to reap the fruits of your actions. All the great bibles agree here.

Once my Master said, "Stand there." We were talking about destiny. I stood. He said, "Will you please lift one foot off the ground?" And I lifted my foot. He said, "Now lift both feet off the ground." I said, "I'm sorry, I cannot do it." He thus taught me that 50% of your destiny is in your hands and 50% is with Providence. Will you please play your part so that Providence helps you?

What do we do? We get so involved that we forget our duties. A human being has immense capacity and when he taps that capacity, he can be free from all these bondages. Then he is the creator of his own destiny. Otherwise destiny leads him adrift like dry leaves blown by the wind creating many patterns against the sky. That is not our human destiny. A human being is a perfect being though still incomplete. If he learns to complete himself then there is nothing higher than that.

Your body is connected to your thinking portion, conscious and unconscious mind, with the help of these two guards called inhalation and exhalation. Now, when conscious mind, breath, and body separate from the unconscious mind and soul, it is called death. Separation is called death. Even after death, you carry all the past memories and all your desires in your unconscious mind. It's like a car, a vehicle, which you drive wherever you go. You are still an individual. When you take off your garment in the bathroom where do you go? When you take off the pillow cover, where does the pillow go? Take off the book cover, where does the book go? It remains there, no problem. The soul is immortal. Soul is like a ripple in the vast ocean of bliss. It comes from that ocean, it plays in the ocean and it subsides in the ocean. It does not go anywhere. It has risen from the ocean as a ripple, and it goes back into the ocean. There are many desires hidden in the unconscious mind. Those desires are responsible for your coming back to this world. You have certain desires

to fulfill. Those desires motivate you to come forward, and
you need a conscious mind, you need breath and you need
a body, all of which you assume again. The day this vehicle is dropped, that is called emancipation and complete
freedom. Otherwise you are still an individual. Just as all
these people are wearing different colors of garments according to their desire, you assume a body according to
unfulfilled desires. Parents and children pick each other,
wife and husband pick each other, to fulfill their desires.

There are two words, the word rebirth and the word
reincarnation. In English, you have only one word, birth.
Sanskrit has some beauty, in Sanskrit there are two words:
janma and *shrishti*. What is janma? *Janit pradhurbhave*. You
don't see me. This is called janma. I was there, I have come
forward. I was in the unseen world, I came forward. That's
called janma, rebirth. You are already there and you came
forward, that's called rebirth. So from the unknown to
the known and from the known to the unknown, you are
going through two gates. One is called birth, the other is
called death. What is reincarnation? In this lifetime you
want to serve, you have examined all aspects of life. One
day you decide that selfless service to humanity is the greatest of all duties. "I don't want to be liberated, I don't want
to be selfish. If I am liberated and you are in bondage,
what good is that life? I don't want to live that way, no. I
will come back again and serve my people, all people." So
that desire brings you back to the world, and that is called
reincarnation. And you serve people because selfless service is such an exact prayer that nobody can deny.

I also believe in this prayer of selfless service, the
greatest of all prayers. You don't expect anything, you
just serve. Why? Because that is the only way for liberat-
ing others. Therefore you learn to do this. Reincarnation

is for that human being who has no desires for himself, but who wants to serve others, lead others. Such human beings are reincarnated to help the masses.

Now, one by one we will touch three levels. How to be free from the bondage of karma? That is universal bondage. It is an accepted fact that as you sow, so shall you reap. Here all the great religions meet. There is no dispute on it. Though Jesus didn't teach it, he didn't deny it either. A lot of time is wasted brooding on karma and reincarnation so Jesus thought it's useless to teach it. He was not wrong. If you go on thinking about your past reincarnations, your present is gone. He was right. There are many paths and all paths lead to one summit. Don't condemn your path. I know the Bible better than any other book, I have studied it so deeply.

A human being cannot live without doing karma, actions. And when he does some karma he reaps the fruits of the actions. And those fruits lead him to do more actions and there is no end. He creates a whirlpool for himself and he cannot come out of that. Is there any way that you go on doing your actions and yet remain free from the bondage of karma? I say yes. If you grease your karma with love, then you will not have a problem. You have stress today, "My wife doesn't listen to me." She thinks, "My husband doesn't listen to me." They both are going through self-created stress. But if you simply change the concept, there will be no stress. Stress has become the biggest killer today. Everybody says I have stress, I have stress. Why do you have stress? Wife wants to control the husband, husband wants to control the wife. Why do you want to control anyone? This tussle is going on all the time, in all families and you call it family life and love. When I come to your home, you all smile. When I go outside, then you start fighting. I know that and I understand. I think there can be harmony in the family if there is understanding, understanding on a higher level.

A man in bondage cannot think right. A man in bondage is a slave. A slave has no choice. How to be free from that? If I go on doing my duties, and I give the fruits of my actions to others, I will be free. Where are you committing a mistake? You are not giving up the fruits of your actions though you are doing your duties. Why do you do charity, tell me? You do charity because you think, "I will have a good name." Then another level of charity, "If I do charity my ego will be cleansed. If I do charity I will get double that in my next lifetime." Actually, why do you want to do charity? You want to do charity because you are holding on to something. Give away the fruits and be free.

Thus comes freedom from the bondage of karma. There will be no bondage. We are all doing our actions but for others and renouncing the fruit. That's why the family unit was created. The husband does actions for his wife, his wife for him and both do for their children and they in turn do for other children. So the family is meant to radiate love to all, not hatred. We have to start at home. We should create our family in such a way so that it radiates love.

After having this freedom from the bondage, there is another freedom that we need, confusion created by the mind. You know what is confusion? Very close to profusion. Profusion creates confusion. If you have twenty things to do, you are confused. If you have a few things to do, you will be not confused. Don't give too much work to yourself. Have 100 things and you cannot manage anything. Let us make a practical formula for practice. All the things in the world, no doubt are meant for you. Enjoy them. But are they yours? No. So don't get attached to them. Early in the morning, tell yourself, "All the things of the world are meant for me, I will enjoy them, but I have no right to get attached to them by owning them, by possessing them. My wife is for me, my children are for me, my house is for me. But they are not mine, there is no attachment." This formula should be made and practiced in daily life. Again I'm repeating, all the things of the world belong to Providence. They are given to you. Use them but do not get attached to them. "I cannot be attached to them, for they are not mine, but I am using them." With this formula you are free from the bondage of karma. Practice it everyday, at least one day, and just see how much delight you experience.

Now there is one saying of the scriptures, why are you afraid of me and why am I afraid of you? *Dvitiyadvai bhayam bhavati.* I think you are different from me, I am different from you, we are afraid of each other. But the moment I come to know that we are only one, I will never be afraid of you. Here I give an example. At night, my two fingers which are very powerful do not hurt my eyes. My teeth do not bite my tongue unless I am sick. Why? Because all the limbs have the understanding that we belong to only one. The day we form the understanding that we all belong to only one reality, we will not have any conflict. We are living in an unnatural way, that is why we are suffering. This suffering is self-created. And, how can God help you? I cried, I said, "God help me, help me." He said, "Son, you create problems for yourself. How can I help you? Please help yourself." I cried. I said, "Somehow or other change my mind." He said, "Your mind is yours, you have to change it yourself." Human efforts have to be made. When human effort is complete and you cannot do anything, then you cry for help and help comes from Providence. This is truth.

Freedom comes in gradual steps, or sometimes it comes suddenly as in the case of Valmiki or St. Paul. There is no limit to grace. But grace dawns when you have accomplished your mission in life, when you have made all the efforts. In the ancient scriptures called the Vedas, there was a great rishi called Karnava. *Karnav* means one who cried. He made all the efforts but he failed. Finally he cried and said, "Lord, I have done my best." Then, suddenly, he realized. Let us do our best without expecting the results. Results are bound to come, for every action has its reaction.

After every day there is a night and after every night there is a day. This is going on for ages. We are in the night awaiting the day. Let us prepare ourselves, with the hope that our next generation will see light and not follow the darkness. There is always hope and we should live with that hope. That's why the Upanishads say, *uttishtata jagrata praptavaranya bodhasa.* Wake up, remain awake and gain that knowledge which liberates you. All great men come according to their times, do their work and go, it's team work. One comes, another comes, this is team work. Rama gave a message. Krishna gave a different message according to the times. Mohammed gave one message in the morning, another in the afternoon, yet another in the evening. There is no conflict, there is no difference, for they have all come to enlighten us, to help humanity.

You must have heard two names, famous names in the West, they were great men. One was Darwin and another was Huxley. Darwin and Huxley did not believe in God, but they were great men. One of the priests of a meditative order got confused. "They were great men no doubt," he thought, "but they did not believe in God. Let me see what has happened to them." So in deep meditation he went to heaven. Here the guard stopped him saying, "You mortal, I don't find your name on our list. How come you are here?" He said, "I want to see your list, to see if you have two people with you." The guard said, "Get out of this place. I won't show you my list." The priest said, "Look, people in heaven are gentle and kind. So you must be a gentle and good person." He praised the guard and the guard said, "Ok, here is the list." They did not have the names of Huxley and Darwin on that list. The priest was very bothered. He said, "Which is the way to hell?" The guard said, "Look at that hell hole, go through it." The priest went through it. There he found a huge person standing outside who said, "Hey, who are you?" He said, "Sir, I have come from the mortal world. I want to know whether Huxley and Darwin are here, as they are not in heaven." He saw a gate that was unique, superior to that of heaven, and beautiful gardens. It was so wonderful. The priest asked, "Is this hell or heaven?" The guard replied, "Go and ask Huxley and Darwin, they are walking in the garden." So the priest approached them, "Sir, good morning to you." They said, "Good morning." "Sir, is it hell or heaven?" They said, "It was hell alright when we came here. But with all our might and intelligence we created a heaven out of it."

Any creative person can convert hell into heaven. This is the point. You have to do it, you can do it, you should do it. So, heaven and hell are here, let us create that harmony, that symphony which helps us, by understanding life, understanding each other, learning to love each other, discharging our duties, being nice to the neighbors, to the country, to the whole of humanity. Again I say, O human being, you are God all right, learn to be a good human. Make that effort.

I was brought up by a great man, a sage born in Bengal who lived for many, many years in the mountains. Our country will perhaps never have a yogi like him for 200-300 years. I'm not praising him because he was my Master. He was a man of great wisdom and knowledge. In my childhood I became an orphan and was taken by my Master, who educated me in modern universities as well as in the monasteries of the Himalayas. I think we human beings are not trained, so we waste our time and energy thinking about others and not thinking about ourselves. My Master always used to say, "Mind your own business. Know thyself on all levels, the way you think, the way you breathe, the way you function in the external world, and that will help you and will prevent you from wasting your time." The final word, my Master gave me, "I send you to the West to share my knowledge, it's not yours. You are only a messenger."

My Master brought me up from the age of three, a child who did not see his parents, who did not have brothers, sisters, or anyone. He brings up this child and never spanks him and never takes anything, not even a glass of water from him. I started crying. He said, "Why are you crying?" I said, "You have not taken any service from me." He laughed. So I rushed to the mountains, in the Himalayas, and there was a beautiful blue lotus coming out of the rock. I pulled it out and straightaway ran to him. He started crying. He said, "You have killed a child of nature. Why did you do this? Being my son you have done this?" Since then, I never accept flowers no matter from where they come. I don't pluck flowers. He told me, "Go into the world. Teach your students with the same zeal with which I taught you." That is my *dakshina*, that is my love offering. I am trying my best, but I fail sometimes and sometimes I am successful.

I always believe in maintaining a state of joy by remembering the Lord's name. You know what Guru Nanak Dev said in simple layman's language? *Nanak dukhiya sab sansara sukhiya soyjo nama adhara.* Nobody has seen God, O Nanak. The whole world is in a state of chaos, happy is he, who remembers the Lord's name with every breath of his life.

I pray to the divinity in you. I thank you very much but all the praises go to the Lord of life. A human being is not worthy of such praise.

And if from these lips while here I dwelt,
A heedless taunt you ever have felt,
Forgive me, forget, and now adieu,
I bid goodbye to all of you.

Peace, peace, peace.

APPENDIX A

Diaphragmatic Breathing

Although breathing is one of our most vital functions, it is little understood and often done improperly. Most people breathe in a shallow and haphazard manner, going against the natural rhythmic movement of the body's respiratory system. Diaphragmatic breathing, on the other hand, promotes a natural, even movement of breath that strengthens the nervous system and relaxes the body.

The principal muscle of diaphragmatic breathing, the diaphragm, is a strong, horizontal, dome-shaped muscle. It divides the thoracic cavity, which contains the heart and lungs, from the abdominal cavity, which contains the organs of digestion, reproduction, and excretion. The diaphragm is located approximately two finger-widths below the nipples in its relaxed or dome-shaped state. It comes up slightly higher on the right side (between the fourth and fifth ribs) than it does on the left side (between the fifth and sixth ribs). In the center the diaphragm is located at the xiphoid process, the lower part of the sternum. The rectus abdominus, the two strong vertical muscles of the abdomen, work in cooperation with the diaphragm during diaphragmatic breathing.

During inhalation the diaphragm contracts and flattens; it pushes downward, causing the upper abdominal muscles to relax and extend slightly and the lower "floating" ribs to flare slightly outward. In this position the lungs expand, creating a partial vacuum, which draws air into the chest cavity. During exhalation the diaphragm relaxes and returns to its dome-shaped position. During this upward movement the upper abdominal muscles contract, and carbon dioxide is forced from the lungs.

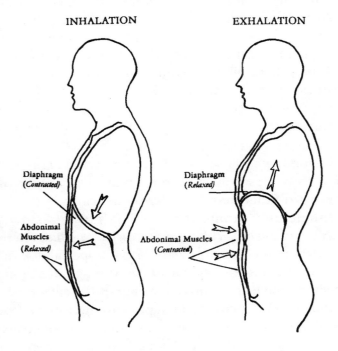

Diaphragmatic breathing has three important effects on the body:

1.   In diaphragmatic breathing, unlike shallow breathing, the lungs fill completely, providing the body with sufficient oxygen.

2.   Diaphragmatic breathing forces the waste product of the respiratory process, carbon dioxide, from the lungs. When breathing shallowly some carbon dioxide may remain trapped in the lungs, causing fatigue and nervousness.

3.   The up and down motion of the diaphragm gently massages the abdominal organs; this increases circulation to these organs and thus aids in their functioning.

In diaphragmatic breathing a minimum amount of effort is used to receive a maximum amount of air; thus, it is our most efficient method of breathing.

Technique

Lie on the back with the feet a comfortable distance apart. Gently close the eyes and place one hand at the base of the rib cage and the other on the chest.

Inhale and exhale through the nostrils slowly, smoothly, and evenly, with no noise, jerks, or pauses in the breath. While inhaling, be aware of the upper abdominal muscles expanding and the lower ribs flaring out slightly. There should be little or no movement of the chest.

Practice this method of deep breathing three to five minutes daily, until you clearly understand the movement of the diaphragm and the upper abdominal muscles. The body is designed to breathe diaphragmatically as is clearly observed in a newborn infant. It should again become natural and spontaneous.

APPENDIX B

Yoga Nidra

Yoga nidra is a simple method consisting of a few breathing and mental exercises. To practice it, lie down on your back in the corpse posture (*shavasana*) in a quiet and undisturbed place, using a pillow and covering yourself with a blanket. The surface should be hard, and the pillow should be soft. Start doing diaphragmatic breathing. After twenty inhalations and exhalations, as you inhale, visualize an incoming wave of the ocean and as you exhale visualize the wave going back into the ocean. After ten or fifteen breaths, the *shavayatra* or 61 points exercise should be carefully done.

Then learn to divest yourself of thoughts, feelings, and desires, but see that you do not touch the brink of sleep. The space between the two breasts, which is called *anahata chakra*, is the center where the mind rests during this practice. The mind should be focused on inhalation and exhalation only. While exhaling, the mind and breath are coordinated in a perfect manner. The mind observes that the inhalation and exhalation are functioning harmoniously. When the breath does not go through the stress of jerks and shallowness, and there is no unconscious expansion of the pause between inhalation and exhalation, then it establishes harmony. Beginners, for lack of practice, are trapped by inertia, and in most cases they experience going to the brink of sleep. This should be avoided in all cases. One should not pursue the practice at this state, but should just wake up and then repeat the same process the next day. This practice of emptying yourself and focusing on the breath should not be continued for more than ten minutes in the beginning, and it should not be practiced more than once a day, for the mind has a habit of repeating its experience, both unconsciously and consciously. In habit formation, regularity, punctuality, and a systematic way of practice should be followed literally.

Technique

Lie in shavasana; relax completely for one to two minutes. Bring your attention to the point between the eyebrows and think of the number "1." Keep the attention fixed on that point for one to two seconds. In the same manner, continue concentrating on the points and corresponding numbers through point 31.

Repeat the exercise twice. Practice for seven to ten days. When this exercise can be done without allowing the mind to wander, then continue through all 61 points.

Practice the 61 points exercise after relaxation and before pranayama. The exercise may be begun on either the right or left side, but be consistent. If you begin (on the torso) with the right arm, then in the lower extremities also begin with the right leg. Sixty-one points should not be practiced when you feel sleepy or tired.

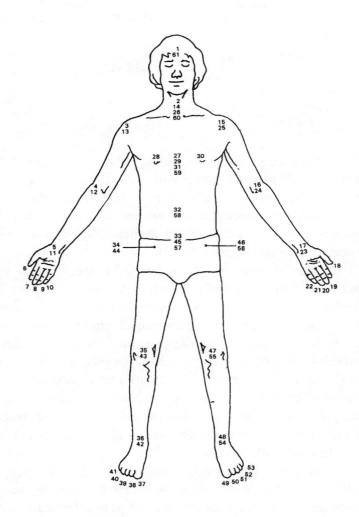

Shavayatra, 61 Points

APPENDIX C

Agni Sara

Agni sara means "energizing the solar system," the area of the body associated with digestion. Agni sara also benefits the bowels, bladder, digestive system, nervous system, circulatory system, and reproductive system. Of all the exercises, this one is the most beneficial, and if time is very short, it may be performed only.

This exercise can be performed correctly only after discriminating between the abdominal and pelvic regions of the body. 'Abdomen' is a general term for the large area extending from the diaphragm muscle down to the base of the trunk. The abdominal region is protected by two strong muscles, the abdominus recti muscles. The lowest portion of the abdomen is more specifically called the pelvis. The pelvis extends from a line slightly below the navel down to the pubic bone. The muscles of the pelvis may be contracted separately from the muscles in the higher navel and abdominal regions.

Note: It is for the above reason that the following exercise, agni sara, differs from the exercise commonly taught in beginning hatha yoga classes and given the same name. That exercise is actually a simple variation of the stomach lift and will not give the benefits described here.

Practice

Standing with the feet comfortably apart, the knees slightly bent, rest the weight of the body with your hands on your knees. As you exhale, draw the pelvic area inward and up. Continue to contract this area as long as the exhalation continues. There is no retention of breath. As the inhalation begins, slowly release the contraction and let the pelvic muscles relax. Continue this systematic contraction and relaxation with each breath. If you tire or become short of breath, pause and breathe freely before continuing. Start with ten breaths. Gradually increase to as many as fifty breaths, or more.

It may take many months to acquire the control and stamina necessary to perform this exercise correctly. Do not become discouraged. Your efforts will be rewarded with excellent health.

APPENDIX D

Sushumna Application

For meditation you have to establish tranquility. And for that, the system is to apply sushumna, a simple method of breath awareness. To begin the process of sushumna awakening, ask your mind to focus on the space between the two nostrils, where the nose meets the space above the upper lip. Focus the mind on the breath as it flows past this point. This first step in learning sushumna application is learning to change the flow of your breath with your mental ability. To accomplish this process you must learn to create a relaxed focus on the right or left nostril. If the nostril is blocked, then when the mind focuses on it, that nostril will become active. When you have learned to mentally change the flow of the breath in the nostrils, then, a time comes when both nostrils begin to flow evenly. This may take some months or even a year, depending on your capacity and the burning desire within you. When both nostrils flow freely, that is called sandhya, the wedding of the sun and moon, or ida and pingala. Once this experience can be maintained for five minutes, the student has crossed a great barrier, and the mind has attained some one-pointedness and becomes focused inward. When the nostrils flow evenly, the mind cannot worry because it is disconnected from the senses. Then, mind attains a state of joy that is conducive to deep meditation.

About the Author

Swami Rama was born in the Himalayas in 1925. He was initiated by his master into many yogic practices. In addition, Swamiji's master sent him to other yogis and adepts of the Himalayas to gain new perspectives and insights into the ancient teachings. At the young age of twenty-four he was installed as the Shankaracharya of Karvirpitham in South India. Swamiji relinquished this position to pursue intense sadhana in the caves of the Himalayas. Having successfully completed this sadhana, he was directed by his master to go to Japan and to the West in order to illustrate the scientific basis of the ancient yogic practices. At the Menninger Foundation in Topeka, Kansas, Swamiji convincingly demonstrated the capacity of the mind to control so-called involuntary physiological parameters such as heart rate, temperature and brain waves.

Swamiji's work in the United States continued for twenty-three years and in this period he established the Himalayan International Institute of Yoga Science and Philosophy of the USA. Swamiji became well recognized in the US as a yogi, teacher, philosopher, poet, humanist and philanthropist. His models of preventive medicine, holistic health and stress management have permeated the mainstream of western medicine.

In 1989 Swamiji returned to India where he established the Himalayan Institute Hospital Trust in the foothills of the Garhwal Himalayas. Swamiji left this physical plane in November, 1996, but the seeds he has sown continue to sprout, bloom, and bear fruit. His teachings embodied in the words "Love, Serve, Remember" continue to inspire the many students whose good fortune it was to come in contact with such an accomplished, selfless, and loving master.

Himalayan Institute Hospital Trust

The Himalayan Institute Hospital Trust was founded in 1989 by Swami Rama. It continues to grow through his extraordinary grace.

It includes one of the best equipped, modern hospitals in Asia, a medical college with extremely high standards, a nursing school, and mobile clinics and satellite centers to serve the many outlying villages.

Unique are its focus on preventive and curative health care, and on evolving a new pattern of medical education and health care by incorporating the spiritual basis of life in relation to health and modern technology.

Most important, many of the 15 million people in the region who have faced suffering with little or no health care can now look forward to having access to modern healthcare services for themselves and their families.

For information contact:
Himalayan Institute Hospital Trust
Swami Rama Nagar, P.O. Doiwala
Distt. Dehradun-248140, Uttaranchal, India
Phone: 91-135-412081, Fax: 0135-412008
e-mail: hihtpb@sancharnet.in, www. hihtindia.com